Sai Baba a

Sai Baba and Aai

Nikhil Kripalani

YogiImpressions®

YogiImpressions®

SAI BABA AND AAI
First published in India in 2021 by
Yogi Impressions LLP
1711, Centre 1, World Trade Centre,
Cuffe Parade, Mumbai 400 005, India.
Website: www.yogiimpressions.com

First Edition, August 2021

ISBN 978-81-949674-0-8

Printed at: Thomson Press, (I) Ltd., Delhi

Contents

Introduction

A few years ago, a good friend of mine asked me meet an astrologer fondly known as Masterjee. She described him as a cute old man who chewed betel leaf and worked from an office at the back of a hotel in Candolim, Goa. I was immediately curious as to what an astrologer would be doing inside a hotel and, moreover, her description of him made him sound like a character straight out of one of my favourite childhood novels, the 'Malgudi Days' series by R K Narayan.

When I went to meet Masterjee, I had a very pleasant experience and felt as if I had been transported into the world of R K Narayan's stories. Masterjee read my astrological chart very accurately, and I asked for an appointment for my mother to have a reading with him the next day.

During the session with my mother, he happened to tell her with conviction that his wife was very saintly and a devotee of Sai Baba of Shirdi. She had been connected with Baba since the age of five and been blessed with many dreams and visions. I was intrigued to hear about his wife, who everyone addressed as Aai though, at that time, I didn't know much about Sai Baba.

The following day, I asked Masterjee if I could have a chance to meet Aai and gain her blessings. He said he would take her permission first and, if she agreed, I could certainly see her. He told us that she usually spoke very little and kept to herself. I was very excited as I knew this was a rare opportunity to meet a devotee as special as Aai.

About a week later, Aai gave her consent, and I went to visit them at their home. The home had images of Baba in various corners and there was a certain peace that emanated from there. At that time, I did not speak Konkani or Marathi fluently, so Masterjee translated and coordinated our communication. I found a beautiful simplicity about being in Aai's presence.

Over the next two years, I would frequently visit Aai and felt very drawn to her. During this time, she related some anecdotes from her life and shared her experiences with Baba. I was also blessed with some of my own personal experiences of Him. My dear friend and spiritual guide, Gautam Sachdeva, then suggested that all of these anecdotes should be compiled into a book that could inspire devotees of Sai Baba since Aai's life is testimony to

Baba's everpresent grace and she is an instrument through whom He operates.

This book contains the most important incidents and miracles of Baba in Aai's life. Each of these stories clearly shows how Baba continues to steer and guide us, and is always overseeing the welfare of His devotees. Some stories display instances of miracles in which Aai has forewarned people of incidents that have come true to the last word. Of course, in all humility, she attributes everything to Baba and acknowledges Him as the sole doer of all actions.

A little about Masterjee: Although his ancestors were devotees of Baba and had been blessed by His physical darshan, Masterjee himself was not a devout follower of Baba initially. However, after meeting Aai, Baba turned his life around and, soon, his whole life began to revolve around Baba in some way or another. Baba had even miraculously cured his father of asthma, and this leela is shared later in the book.

Masterjee was a schoolteacher by profession and began the study of astrology during his early years of teaching. In time, he became quite proficient with the practice and once he retired, he devoted all his time to being an astrologer.

In the early days of meeting Aai and hearing about the miracles, I was enchanted and occasionally, taken aback with astonishment. Then I had my very own experience in which Aai told me something that soon came to pass.

In the first chapter, I narrate this experience that took place in my second meeting with Aai.

The Dussehra Forewarning

One day, I was leaving my home to seek darshan of my Guruji, Pujya Dharamdas Baba, whose ashram is located in Sihor, Gujarat, and a friend was accompanying me from Goa. En route to the airport, we went to meet Aai and Masterjee to ask for their blessings.

After meeting them, just as we were about to leave, Aai asked me when I would be returning. Before I could reply, Masterjee interrupted, urging us to hurry, and said to Aai, "Let them go, they should not miss their flight."

At this point, I remember Aai telling me, "You will be here on the day of Dussehra." This stands out clearly in my memory because she repeated the statement thrice. Since it is not in my nature to keep track of the days and dates of all holidays, I was unaware of the date of the Dussehra festival or when we would return. We hastened to leave and asked for their blessings; Masterjee gave us some *udi* (sacred ash from Sai Baba's temple in Shirdi) and we set off.

I reached Gujarat and soon settled down at the ashram.

It was a wonderful opportunity and blessing for me to be in the holy presence of my Guru for a few days.

My mother and I used to communicate over the phone and she kept me abreast on the home front as she was taking care of her mother and aunt, both of whom lived with us in Goa.

Over the next few days, she told me that Auntyji's health was not good, and she asked me to speak with her on the phone for it would cheer her up. It was not something to be unduly worried about because Auntyji was prone to indigestion. She occasionally experienced nausea and vomiting that subsided with home remedies. My mother assured me that she would be fine within a day or two.

One evening, when I was sitting in silence at the ashram, I had a very strong urge to check my phone and I excused myself to go upstairs to my room. When I picked up my phone, there was a text message from my mother that said, 'Call me back immediately. Auntyji has passed away.'

While reading the message I intuitively knew that she had a peaceful transition, which my mother confirmed later. Some family members from Mumbai had already left for Goa to be with my mother. However, I was only able to leave the next morning as there were no trains or flights available that night.

It was only at the airport that it struck me that it was Dussehra! I was immediately reminded of Aai's words, "You will be here on the day of Dussehra."

Once I got home, Auntyji's last rites were completed smoothly. Later, the priest told me that it was an auspicious day for Auntyji's transition as Dussehra was also the same day that Sai Baba had taken His *mahasamadhi* (when an enlightened master consciously gives up his mortal body and merges with the Divine). This brought further consolation and a sense of calm for all of us.

When I spoke to Aai about the incident later, she had a smile on her face and did not say much. All she said was, "You were supposed to be here and Baba got you here." She reassured me that this was a good omen and a sign of Baba's presence in my life.

Aai repeatedly says that everything that happens through her is only Baba's doing and she has no awareness about these actions. All she encourages devotees to do is to love Him like one loves their mother, to build a relationship with Him and to rely on Him for everything. She says then one will begin to experience Baba's grace and care.

ॐ

The next few chapters explore the early days of Masterjee and Aai's life, how they became devotees of Baba and how their lives were miraculously interwoven with each other's through Baba's grace.

How Aai Was First Drawn To Baba As A Child

Aai's connection with Baba – in this lifetime – started during her childhood at the tender age of five when she first saw a statue of Him at her aunt's home. "Sai Baba performed many miracles and we have felt blessed by Him," her aunt said when Aai asked about Him. Aai enjoyed visiting her aunt and listening to tales of Baba. Soon after that, someone gave her a *pothi* (small prayer book) of Sai Baba so that she could pray to Him too.

At that time, a girl named Anusaya lived in Aai's neighbourhood who had suffered from some type of mental trauma and lost the ability to speak coherently. She had become aggressive and used to scream violently at random intervals. Her family took her to numerous doctors and priests, and tried various things to cure her but nothing helped. Anusaya's sister was Aai's friend and both the girls had the small pothi of Sai Baba. With childlike faith, they thought that if they touched the pothi to Anusaya's forehead, she would be cured.

Firmly clasping the pothi, they tried to place it on her forehead, but the girl got hostile and didn't let them approach her. They then tried to get her to recite the mantra 'Sai Ram' by asking her to repeat it after them.

Anusaya got even more agitated. Aai and her friend started reciting 'Sai Ram' over and over again. They did not have any feelings of devotion, but innocently believed that it would be good for the girl if she recited this mantra.

Then something bizarre happened; when she heard the chanting Anusaya became unconscious. Her mother came running and asked Aai, "What did you do to her?" Aai replied, "We did not do anything. We were just reciting Baba's name and suddenly Anusaya fainted."

Then Anusaya gestured to her mother, asking for a notebook and a pen to write. Everyone in the room was alert and knew that something unusual was happening. Aai told Anusaya, "Since you are unable to say it, write down Baba's name."

Anusaya took the pen and wrote 'S' a few times in Marathi. She could not manage more than that. She tried once again but it was fruitless. Then, Aai asked her to wait a while before attempting to write again. The next time, she wrote down 'Sa' a few times and eventually managed to write the complete word 'Sai'. Everyone was delighted!

Within a few months, the girl slowly recovered and was able to speak. She eventually finished her college and went on to lead a normal life. This incident planted the seeds of faith and devotion in Aai as this was the first time she had witnessed Baba's miracle take place in front of her at a very young age.

The photograph of Baba that Aai would worship

Aai's First Divine Vision

Aai's childhood was spent in Malwan (a town in the western state of Maharashtra), where she looked after her mother (who had become mentally disturbed after Aai's father passed away) and went to school.

It was Shivratri and ten-year-old Aai was fasting like everyone else at home. That evening, she and her friend were walking towards the sea shore when, all of a sudden, both of them saw a vision of Shiva and Parvati. Aai grew animated and started telling the people around them to catch sight of the God and Goddess too. However, nobody other than Aai and her friend could see them.

They began moving towards the divine vision but could not get closer. With folded hands, the two girls chanted, 'Shiva Shankar, Parvati', and continued to follow the vision. The onlookers thought they had gone crazy.

They chased the vision down the road but it eluded them. Eventually they saw it vanish into the rays of the setting sun, merging with the infinite.

Aai felt that she was only able to see the vision because of her friend, who was a devotee of Lord Shiva. Meanwhile, the friend insisted that she saw it because of Aai. This was Aai's first experience of a divine vision and it was after this that Aai's connection with Sai Baba deepened.

Masterjee's Ancestors Were Blessed By Baba

Similar to how Aai had her direct experiences of Baba from her childhood, Masterjee, too, had his connection with Baba through his father and grandfather who were blessed to have the holy darshan of Baba while He was still in His physical form.

By the year 1910, Sai Baba's popularity was increasing and devotees were flocking to Shirdi to take His holy darshan. Masterjee's father was also drawn to Him.

When he went to Dwarkamayee (the mosque where Baba resided), he saw Baba sitting in the center of a circle, surrounded by His devotees, and smoking a *chillum* (a small pipe used for smoking tobacco). Baba asked Masterjee's father for *dakshina* (offering) of nine rupees and then, suddenly, passed him the chillum to smoke.

Masterjee's father was perplexed and did not know what to do as he had never smoked before. Some of the devotees near Baba then prompted him to take the chillum so as to not offend Baba.

Masterjee's father innocently inhaled from the pipe and then burst into a violent cough! He had suffered from chronic asthma since his childhood and the smoke from the chillum triggered his ceaseless bout of coughing.

Seeing this, Baba gave him a hard thump on his back and the cough stopped immediately. What happened thereafter was truly miraculous: his asthma vanished completely, never to bother him again!

When Masterjee's grandfather heard about this leela, he too wished to meet Sai Baba and have His holy darshan. On his first visit itself, Baba blessed Masterjee's grandfather and gave him two rupees as prasad. Baba also remarked that Masterjee's grandfather was a great *Bhagwad bhakt* (a devotee who has immersed himself in the teachings of the sacred Bhagwad Gita) which was a big honour for him.

In time, after receiving Baba's blessings, Masterjee's grandfather received a sudden promotion in his career and became the deputy collector of the Nashik district (a major town next to Shirdi, in the state of Maharashtra) which was considered to be a very prestigious position.

ॐ

Later, after taking darshan of Baba, Masterjee's father went up to Him and requested an initiation. Baba told him,

"You have already been given an *updesh* (initiation) why are you asking me again?"

Masterjee's father was confused. Initially he did not understand what Baba meant, but as he recollected an incident from the past, he was humbled by the all-knowingness of Baba!

When he was 12 years old, he was bathing in the Krishna River with his friend. When they climbed out of the water, a saint approached them and whispered a mantra into their ears as a form of initiation. This event was forgotten with the passage of time until he was reminded of it by Baba.

Masterjee's parents and grandparents were indeed blessed to have met Sai Baba when He was physically alive and they continued worshipping Him even after they shifted to Jamkhandi (a city in the southern state of Karnataka) from their childhood home in the state of Maharashtra.

However, some of the elders in their family objected to this veneration because they were a traditional Hindu Brahmin family and Baba was considered to be a Muslim saint by many people at the time. Masterjee's grandfather payed no heed to this, and placed the photograph of Sai Baba in a suitcase from where they worshipped Him privately until their very last breath.

ॐ

When Masterjee was a young boy, he saw the photograph of Baba which his father had and, with the candidness of a child, asked him, "Why do you worship this old man? Who is He?" His father, who was generally known for being calm and even tempered, got very agitated. He corrected Masterjee sternly and said, "Don't ever refer to Him as an old man! Baba is Eternity incarnate. One day, your whole world will revolve around His name!"

In time, Masterjee's father's words would come true and, especially after marrying Aai, Masterjee's whole life would begin to revolve around Sai Baba. He would also help spread Baba's name far and wide by sharing Baba's leelas and Aai's experiences with the people who came to him for astrology readings, thereby inspiring and impacting numerous other devotees.

How Aai And Masterjee Got Married

Masterjee was very close to his grandfather and always carried his picture in his wallet. In his youth, Masterjee studied in a law college in Mumbai (a large city in Maharashtra) with the intention of starting his own practice one day.

However, when he graduated from law school, his grandfather suddenly passed away. This affected him greatly, and he became depressed and withdrawn. His family felt that if he got engaged in work, it would help him get over the loss and move forward in his life. Initially, he found a few odd jobs but nothing seemed to appeal to him, and he remained disinterested and disengaged from the world.

After a series of strange coincidences, he landed up in Kolhapur (a city over 300km away from Mumbai but in the same state) and was then sent to Malwan (the same town in Maharashtra where Aai lived) where he got a job in a school as an English teacher. After finding a place to stay, he got involved in his teaching routine but could not stop grieving about his grandfather.

Word quickly spread that Masterjee was also an astrologer, and one morning, a man who lived opposite the school requested him to read his family's horoscopes. Masterjee agreed to visit their home that afternoon.

It was a large home and they appeared to be an affluent family who were well-known traders and exporters of cashew nuts. Masterjee was given five horoscopes to read and the family members seemed very pleased to hear his interpretations.

The lady of the house then sat alone with Masterjee and asked him to read the last horoscope in detail. "Tell me when this person will get married," she said.

By then, Masterjee's mind had strayed to thoughts of his grandfather and he felt distracted. After a superficial glance at the chart, he replied, "In about two months."

"Are you speaking the truth? Is she really going to get married?" she asked incredulously.

Masterjee was puzzled. "Tai, why are you asking me this? Is there a problem?"

"No, no, please check the horoscope properly!" The woman replied.

To Masterjee's dismay, when he read the chart once again, he realised that the woman in question was about 43 years old.

Putting on a brave front and trusting his own skill, he replied, "Tai, whatever I have told you is going to happen; she is going to get married. Age is not a concern, even if she is 60 or 70, it is going to happen."*

The woman was very thrilled to hear this. She asked Masterjee to stay for refreshments and went inside. A few minutes later, a young girl who worked there entered the room carrying a tray with tea and snacks.

What took place next was a miraculous, life-changing occurrence. Masterjee and the young girl were the only two present in the room. When the girl placed the tray on the table, Masterjee suddenly grasped her hand and uttered, "Will you marry me?"

"Yes", she said simply, and quickly left the room.

Masterjee was in a state of shock and disbelief about what had just happened. He had no idea what had come over him and caused him to act that way.

He was remorseful and wanted to apologise to the girl for his impudence. The next day, he happened to meet her in the market and said, "I am very sorry, I do not know what happened yesterday. I do not even know your name and I offended you; please forgive me."

To this, Aai replied, "No, no, it is already decided. Before you came to me, I had a dream in which an old man asked me to take care of his grandson!"

Masterjee was startled to hear this. He opened his wallet and showed her his grandfather's photograph. She looked at it and confirmed that it was the same man in her dream!

Before this incident took place, Aai was almost engaged to a local young man, but it was found that his character was questionable and the alliance was not pursued. Aai's friends criticised her and said, "What did you do? You lost an opportunity." Aai replied, "My opportunity is coming." And exactly two weeks later, she met Masterjee!

Masterjee subsequently sent a photograph of Aai to his father and wrote to him about what had happened. His father approved and wrote back, "Meena (Aai's real name) is a great devotee of Baba. Everything will be in perfect order. Get married immediately."

Before agreeing to the marriage, Aai put forth just two conditions that Masterjee would have to accept. The first one was that her mother, who was not in sound mental health, would always live with them, and the second one, was that Baba would always be her priority over everything else in life.

Masterjee happily agreed and supported her wholeheartedly in both her wishes. They were married by April 1960, within a year of their first meeting.

ॐ

** Masterjee's prediction came true and the lady in question did get married within two months.*

When Masterjee narrates the story of their meeting, listeners are mesmerised. He did not know Aai's name, age, caste, or family before proposing to her. It was all preordained; it was Baba's wish.

The photograph of Masterjee's grandfather that he would always carry with him

Aai's First Visit To Shirdi

In 1972, Aai was going to Shirdi for the first time. Though she had a deep connection with Baba since childhood, circumstances and challenges prevented her from visiting Shirdi until then.

Masterjee, who had been to Shirdi before, would be accompanying his family for their first trip together, which he had funded after taking a small loan from the bank.

Unaware that they could take a bus from Goa to Pune directly, they first went to Belgaum, which is two hours from Goa, from where they would board a train to Pune. A bus would then take them to Shirdi from Pune.

In Belgaum, they found accommodation in a cheap guesthouse called Amba Bhavan, about a kilometre and a half away from the railway station. The guesthouse was largely unoccupied and they made themselves comfortable. They informed the manager and security guard that they wished to go to Shirdi via Pune the next day. They were told that there was an early morning train for Pune, which left at about 4.00 a.m., and were advised to leave for the railway station in the middle of the night. From Pune, they could take a bus to reach Shirdi the following day. Since they did not have an alarm clock, they requested that someone knock at their door and wake them up on time.

Tired after their journey from Goa, they went to sleep soon after dinner. In the middle of the night, Aai was woken by a loud voice that said to her, "Baby, Baby, get up, it's morning! Wake up, Baby!" Aai was startled hearing this, wondering who could have spoken to her since there had been no knock on the door. However, she immediately got out of bed and checked the time. It was around 3.15 a.m.

She roused Masterjee and the children, and they hastily freshened up and left the hotel. Masterjee said he would like a cup of tea, but Aai insisted they reach the station first since the train would have already arrived. While leaving, they spoke with the guard to inquire about who was in the room next door, and he said there were no occupants in the adjacent rooms!

When they reached the station, Masterjee bought their tickets and went to the stationmaster, who urged them, "Go quickly, the train is about to leave. Board immediately!" They ran towards the train and heard the whistle blow. Sure enough, as soon as they boarded the train, it started to move.

Once they settled down, they reflected on how fortunate

they had been to get this train on time. Who could have woken them up in the middle of the night from their deep sleep? At the lodge, the rooms adjacent to theirs had been vacant. Then they realised that it had been none other than Baba who had woken them up, else they would have surely missed this train!

They arrived in Shirdi at 2.00 a.m. on Amavasya, the first night of Diwali. As they stood on the bus stop wondering how they could reach the temple, they saw an old man and asked him for directions. He began screaming forcefully at Aai, "I am standing here; can't you see me? Can't you see me? I am standing here, go that way!"

Aai wondered who this strange man was giving them directions in such a bizarre way. At that moment, she did not realise that there was more to it. As they walked in the direction indicated by the old man, they turned back only to see that he had vanished. The children wondered if he was a ghost but Aai denied this saying that it was none other than her beloved Baba.

They followed the directions, and safely reached a place to stay. They knew this had only been possible due to Baba's grace and continuous help, and they were very grateful to Him. The next morning they had a wonderful darshan at Baba's samadhi and at Dwarkamayee.

ॐ

This incident is a gentle reminder of one of Baba's promises to His devotees:

"I am ever living to help and guide all, who come to Me, who surrender to Me and who seek refuge in Me."

The Mysterious Train Journey Back Home

A few days into their visit to Shirdi, Aai injured her toe, and soon it became quite painful. She bandaged it and managed to walk about in Shirdi, but it got progressively worse when they left and quickly became acute by the time they reached Pune. Though she was definitely experiencing a lot of discomfort and pain, by nature, Aai never shared her troubles with anyone, especially with Masterjee, as she didn't want him to worry on her account. She would rather suffer in silence than let anyone be inconvenienced because of her.

Masterjee had booked train tickets for their return journey from Pune to Goa, but seeing Aai in pain, he asked her if she would prefer to stay back in Pune until she felt better. Knowing they had limited money, and since Masterjee had already purchased their tickets, she told him that it would be best for them to take the train, as they did not have enough resources to afford accommodation plus buy fresh train tickets the next day. "We have to go," she said simply.

The train was scheduled to depart at 8.00 p.m. and they waited on the platform with the children and the luggage. When the Goa-bound train arrived, all the compartments were full and the train was packed. They ran along the length of the platform, trying to find a suitable bogie but there was just no space for them to enter. It was even more difficult with the children and with Aai's painful toe. They could just watch as the overcrowded train left Pune station.

Disheartened by what happened, Masterjee suggested that they leave the station and take the bus instead. Aai did not approve of this idea either and she reminded him that they had already bought train tickets and that they had very little money for additional travel expenses. Forgetting her own agony, she said they ought to wait for the next train instead.

It was almost 9.30 p.m. They waited at the railway station and took some tea and refreshments after which the children fell asleep. Aai told Masterjee that they would board the next Goa-bound train in the morning. They would explain their situation if anyone asked: They had valid tickets but since the train was full, they weren't able to board it, so were boarding the next available train instead.

A little while later, an old, extremely thin *hamaal*

(porter) appeared. He wore a red, neat, freshly washed porter's uniform and cap. He approached Aai and asked, "Tai, where are you going? To Goa?" She replied, "Yes, but since the train was full, how could we go?"

The hamaal then said, "I will arrange for your seats in a special train; how much will you pay me?"

Aai replied, "We will pay you whatever you want."

"I want two rupees", said the old hamaal.

They agreed and he asked them to wait where they were. He returned after a few minutes and asked them to follow him.

He hoisted their youngest daughter on his shoulder and was about to bend down to pick up a piece of luggage, but seeing that he was old and frail, Aai told him they would manage the luggage themselves.

Masterjee and Aai quickly gathered their bags and walked behind him. They crossed several platforms till they reached the very last one that was empty and desolate, without a soul in sight. There were no lights on this platform, just a solitary train coach waiting on the tracks without even an engine attached.

He then told them, "You want to go to Goa? Get inside; this bogie will take you." He opened the door for them, took his towel off his shoulder, dusted the steps and asked them to climb up and board the coach. He then told them that they would reach Goa undisturbed and they could rest inside without further worry.

After loading their luggage, and placing it below their seats, he left, telling them that he would be back. Masterjee put his hand in his pocket to offer him money, but by then the hamaal was gone.

Aai wondered what was going on. Here they were in an empty coach on a dark platform with no idea of what might happen next. She told Masterjee, "This is an empty bogie, there is no one here, but at least we can spend the night. We shall see in the morning." Saying this, they lay down on the berths and slept. A few hours later, they suddenly felt a thump when the bogie was connected to a train. The train began to move; they were on a journey, but had no idea of the destination.

As the journey progressed, more passengers got in and confirmed what the old hamaal had promised them – they were on their way home to Goa! A few more passengers joined them and one family even offered them a breakfast of parathas. The old hamaal never showed up again and when they made enquiries about him by asking other hamaals about his identification number (it had been a three digit number that stayed in their memory), they were told that no one had that particular badge number! They once again realised that it was nothing but a miracle by Baba. Baba is ever loving and full of compassion to the ones who surrender completely to Him.

ॐ

It was one of Baba's assurances, "Though I be no more in flesh and blood, I shall ever protect My devotees." This incident is one of the innumerable times in which devotees have experienced His grace and protection.

Dust On Baba's Photograph

Once Aai and the family had gone to Masterjee's ancestral home in Jamkhandi and Aai had affectionately brought a photograph of Baba for the home. Once they reached, she put it in the family puja room and asked Masterjee's mother to light an agarbatti and do darshan at least every Thursday.

Masterjee's mother agreed to do so. Masterjee's father was a great devotee of Baba. His mother, however, did not share the same faith. Being an orthodox Brahmin, she was very traditional in her ways. However, to please Aai, she agreed to take care of Baba's photograph with devotion.

After they went back to Goa, Aai's mother-in-law was influenced by her neighbours who questioned why she was worshipping a Muslim saint despite being a Brahmin. This affected her and she put away Baba's photograph in a cupboard.

Soon after this incident, Aai had a dream in which Baba told her, "They have taken Me and put Me on a shelf. A lot of dust has fallen on me; I want to come home."

Aai was deeply disturbed by this dream. Her love for Baba is unimaginable. After narrating the vision to Masterjee in the morning, she asked, "Has your mother done this?" Masterjee denied it, saying his mother was pious and would never do something like that. But Aai continued to feel terribly uncomfortable and asked Masterjee to go to Jamkhandi at once.

The school holidays were over at the new school Masterjee had started teaching in, and he knew he wouldn't be granted leave. He told Aai that he could not go, to which she did not say anything.

He then went to school as usual without thinking too much about the incident. Upon reaching, the school office asked him to submit some original documents. These were important in order to confirm his job application. It was no coincidence that the papers were at his home in Jamkhandi! The school granted him leave for a few days to go and collect the documents.

Masterjee came home and told Aai about what had happened. The next day, he left for Jamkhandi. His mother did not expect to see him back so soon and he went directly to the puja room to check if Baba's photograph was there. To his surprise, he found that the photograph was indeed missing!

Masterjee was agitated and confronted his mother,

"What is this? Why did you remove Baba's photograph?"

His mother replied, "No, no. We were getting disturbed!"

Masterjee said to her, "This is very wrong. My wife had a dream in which Baba told her what you have done."

His mother was stunned after hearing about the dream and felt great remorse. Both of them quickly put Baba's photograph where Aai had placed it and asked for forgiveness.

As time went by, Masterjee's mother's faith in Baba and love towards Aai increased greatly.

Masterjee with his students

Baba Cures Masterjee's Illness

Once there was a celebration at the convent school where Masterjee used to teach and the bishop had come to visit. After the function, the teachers and staff were offered some wine. Masterjee, who had never consumed alcohol before, did not know what to do but his colleagues asked him to quickly drink it so as not to offend the bishop. Masterjee innocently swallowed the contents of his glass and felt a fuzzy, warm sensation in his stomach. It was a strange experience for him.

The next day at school, he felt some pain in his stomach after lunch. Hearing this, one of his colleagues told him that it was due to the drink he had at the previous day's function. "If you have some local cashew liquor, it will help the pain to subside", he advised him.

Ignorant about the consequences of drinking local liquor (since it is highly addictive), Masterjee went with his colleague after school to a local bar. They offered him some local cashew *feni* (a local spirit produced in Goa), which he drank. To his great relief, the pain settled.

Aai had absolutely no idea about alcohol either. She sensed something unusual for Masterjee smelt of liquor when he returned home. She asked him if he had consumed something and Masterjee told her it was a local cashew 'medicinal drink' for his stomach pain. They proceeded to have lunch and forgot about it.

This pattern continued for the next few days. Masterjee would experience stomach cramps around noon and his friends would ask him to accompany them to the local bar where they would have a little cashew feni, after which Masterjee's pain lessened.

This slowly became a ritual and continued for a few weeks until the school closed for the holidays. Then Masterjee developed a mysterious fever. The fever set in at night and subsided by morning. It went on for about two weeks.

Aai was worried and took Masterjee to a local doctor who diagnosed him with an ulcer that needed to be operated upon. He told Aai that Masterjee would need someone to look after him after the surgery, so she should probably inform his parents and ask them to come and help. In addition, the doctor felt that Masterjee might need some blood transfusions after the surgery.

Understandably, Aai was quite anxious and concerned

about this development. Masterjee was the sole breadwinner of the family. Concern for his well-being, plus the additional expenditure, added to Aai's worries and she wondered what they could do. In the meantime, the pattern of fever continued.

Once the school re-opened, Masterjee's desire to drink at that hour persisted. The doctor had given him some medicines for his stomach pain and fever but they did not seem to be helping him.

One night, Aai saw Baba in her dream in which He said to her, "Don't worry, nothing has happened to him. Take him to the doctor who is at his place of work."

Aai was quite astonished and she immediately told Masterjee about the dream and Baba's guidance. She advised him, "There is a doctor where you are working, go and meet him immediately." Masterjee resisted by saying that they were already seeing a doctor but Aai told him to forget about him and enquire about the doctor at school.

The next day at school, he asked the priest, "Father, is there a doctor here at school? I have been experiencing persistent stomach pain and fever and need to see him."

The priest then told him, "Oh, yes, there is a doctor. He is the father of one of your students. I will call that child." The priest then sent for the young boy and instructed him, "Please take Sir to meet your father after school."

The child was delighted at the opportunity and took

Masterjee to his father's clinic. The doctor knew Masterjee was the teacher so he welcomed him and asked how he could be of help. Masterjee then told the doctor about his ailment and the diagnosis of the ulcer. He showed him all the medicines that were prescribed to him by the other doctor. To Masterjee's surprise, the doctor took all of the medicines and threw them into the trash basket.

He then went inside another room, prayed and came back. He told Masterjee that nothing was wrong with him, to which Masterjee once again notified him that he was plagued by fever and pain every night.

The doctor gave Masterjee three aspirin tablets and asked him to take one after every meal and visit him after two days.

Masterjee did as directed and to his surprise, he was free of the pain and fever. As instructed, he went to visit the doctor two days later who told Masterjee, "You are perfectly healthy, you have no ulcer or anything. What has happened is because of your own foolishness. Your body cannot digest alcohol; it is not for you. Do not experiment with these substances again. If you choose not to listen to me, you will lose your health."

Masterjee was very pleased to hear these words. He went home and told Aai what the doctor had told him. Aai then showed him a photograph they had of Baba and pointed out something to him, "See this line, exactly on the stomach, an operation has been done!" In that photograph, white ants had eaten the entire area around Baba's stomach!

The photograph of Baba that was eaten by white ants around the stomach symbolising that He had taken on Masterjee's pain

ॐ

It is interesting how this story came into the book. During the process of interviewing Masterjee and Aai in order to compile anecdotes that they could recollect, they mentioned this tale and photograph of Baba. The photograph has been with Aai for the last 50 years. One day, I requested Masterjee to come with me to Baba's temple in their old home – where their son stays now – so that we could try and locate this particular photograph.

We explored almost every corner but were unable to find it. We gave up all hope and were quite disappointed for it was quite an important photograph. I was very keen to see it and share it with readers. As we were about to leave, something in a corner on a cabinet caught my eye. The object was completely covered with dust and I ran my finger over it. Something made me take a piece of cloth and wipe it clean. What revealed itself was truly miraculous – it was the very same picture frame we had been searching for! Both Masterjee and I were delighted.

Aai's Degree Of Faith

The extent of Aai's devotion to Baba is unfathomable. On one visit to their home, Aai shared that she had delivered all four of her children at home with the help of a midwife. During each birth, Aai had been reading from her pothi right until the time when the baby was born, even during labour pains.

Baba was very particular about the Sadhana of pothi reading, and would not like it if devotees got distracted during their reading to attend to worldy matters. There are numerous accounts in the Sai Satcharita where Baba Himself would ask devotees to first finish their reading and only then come to take His darshan in the mosque.

Aai's religious following of this practice continues to this day. Despite any external circumstance, her Sadhana is undisturbed. This leela is an outstanding example of her dedication to her practices and faith in Baba.

ॐ

When Aai was expecting a child, they had engaged the services of the same nurse who had assisted them during Aai's previous deliveries and lived near their home. When Aai started experiencing labour pains and the nurse was sent for, she was found to be in a drunken slumber. She sleepily muttered, "I'll come tomorrow", and went back to sleep.

Masterjee panicked because they had been counting on this nurse's help and now it seemed there was nobody who could come to their aid at this last minute.

Time was of the essence and a kind neighbour quickly went to fetch an old, blind midwife; it was their only option.

In the middle of the night and with no transport available, the man carried the old midwife on his back and brought her to Aai's home. Luckily, this old lady was greatly experienced in her field and by using her delicate touch she helped Aai deliver the baby.

It was a sheer miracle that a midwife came to their rescue that night and Aai was able to deliver the child safely.

ॐ

Aai emphasises that once Baba takes you in his embrace, He does not let go of you, but cares for you always. This, of course, is graced upon us when we have the kind of love and devotion to Baba that Aai does.

The Bank Loan And Aai's Curse

In the early days, Aai and Masterjee had to face a lot of financial harships and survive on Masterjee's meagre salary of 120 rupees a month. Very often, they found it difficult to even make ends meet. However, Masterjee was generous and overly trusting of everyone, and would often wind up helping others at the cost of his family.

In one such incident, he wished to help a young man set up his own grocery shop. Although he didn't know this person very well, Masterjee went out of his way and helped him get a bank loan of 5000 rupees. Unfamiliar with the procedures and their consequences, he unwittingly became a guarantor of the loan.

Apart from this, Masterjee also helped him get a space on rent and gave him 1200 rupees to set up the shop.

Aai had some jewellery in the bank locker. Without informing or consulting her, Masterjee sold it off to help raise funds for this man. Aai happened to be cleaning the house and found one of her earrings in a pouch at home and asked Masterjee where the other earring was. He told her that he had perhaps forgotten this one at home while the other one was still safe in the bank locker along with her other ornaments. But Aai knew only too well that he had either sold or pawned her jewellery.

What happened thereafter was rather unfortunate. This person absconded with all the money and it was later discovered that he was a known con artist. Aai and Masterjee were left to deal with a bunch of creditors who turned to them.

As guarantor, Masterjee had to pay the monthly instalments on the loan. In addition to this, there was the shop owner who had leased the shop to this man and now came to collect his rent from Masterjee. The scammer had also taken money and goods on credit from some other small business owners that Masterjee knew.

Masterjee had helped set up that man's business in good faith. Little did he know the ungrateful man would leave them in a big financial mess!

Creditors started coming to their home and asking for their money. It was an extremely testing time for the family as they had a meagre monthly income. The bank manager was their friend and, one day, he compassionately suggested, "Why don't you leave this area and run away? I will do my best to write off your loan by declaring you cannot be traced."

Aai flatly refused, saying, "I will pay you every paisa,

maybe little by little, but we will not budge from here. We have not stolen anything. It was our mistake that we trusted that man, but we will pay everyone back irrespective of how difficult it may be."

One day, the shop owner came to demand his money. He was a crude man who knew about Baba's temple in Aai's home. He started screaming outside their home, trying to get everyone's attention. "These people cheat and lie to others, and then worship Him at the same time. It is better you people throw Baba outside and pay back people like us."

Aai was livid and extremely hurt by these words. She screamed at this man and said, "If my husband and I have made a mistake, you are free to tell us what you like, but don't you dare say anything to Baba or about Baba! What is Baba's mistake in this? He has not taken anything from you! You watch out, there will come a day when you will be roaming the streets with coconut shells in your hand, begging for a living!" Aai spontaneously uttered these words to the man who continued to holler outside.

In the coming months, Aai and Masterjee paid off the local businessmen and began the cycle of paying monthly instalments to the bank. Whatever little savings they had were all exhausted during this time of crisis.

About a year from then, a very shabbily dressed man came home and asked to speak to Masterjee. "About what?" Aai asked. "Please ask Masterjee if I can perform for the children in his school and if I can get work there."

Aai then recognised the man. He was the same shopkeeper who had spoken ill about Baba. He had lost everything and was now making a living as a street performer, using puppets made of coconut shells!

Whatever Aai said to the man that day came true to the last word!

Aai's Mother Was Found In Mapusa

Aai and her mother had lead an extremely challenging life faced with many setbacks. After losing her husband, Aai's mother was depressed to such a degree that she had become mentally disturbed.

This made life even more difficult for Aai. While growing up, Aai had to support herself and her mother. In addition to coping with the emotional trauma, she had to deal with a society that was not supportive. After marrying Masterjee, however, it got much better, as he was very compassionate and understanding.

One day, Aai's son, who was a little boy then, was playing with his grandmother and teasing her. In all innocence, he took a stick and threatened her by saying, "I am going to hit you with this."

Frightened, she ran away from home. When Masterjee came home shortly after, he was informed about the incident. At first, they thought she must have gone to some neighbour's home and would return shortly. As time passed and there was no sign of her, they got worried.

Masterjee soon went in search of her and asked many people in the neighbourhood if they had seen her, but no one could provide any information. One person even told him that a woman had fallen into a nearby well and died!

Riding on a scooter, he looked around in the vicinity but did not see her anywhere. They finally filed a 'missing person' report at the police station and returned home. On their way, they met a friend of Masterjee's who suggested they talk to a man who could communicate with spirits. Seeing no harm in this, Masterjee visited him the next day. To his horror, the man told Masterjee that his mother-in-law had died.

A week passed and there was no news; the family was naturally worried. Their enquiries and searches were yielding nothing. Aai then told Masterjee, "Do not worry, she is alive."

That night, Aai had a dream in which her mother was staying in a Hanuman temple. When she told Masterjee about her dream, he asked her which temple it could be. Aai said, "The one in Mapusa (a town around 8 km away from their home in Calangute)."

One of their neighbours, who had been helping them with the search, was going to Mapusa the next day. He said he would visit the Hanuman temple on their behalf.

When he entered the temple, he saw Aai's mother sitting there in a corner, frightened.

The priest then told him, "This old woman has been staying here for a week. She doesn't eat anything. Whatever food we give her, she refuses to touch it.

"She has a packet of biscuits that she hides and says, 'It's for my grandson.' She cannot speak properly and we cannot understand where she is from. She said she is the mother-in-law of some teacher in Calangute."

The kind neighbour then brought Aai's mother back home to them.

A photograph of Aai with her mother and Masterjee

Baba Prevents A Fire Twice

Every night, Aai would diligently read from Baba's pothi. Her days were busy with household chores, so late at night, after everyone went to sleep she sat with her pothi and meditated.

Since she was tired at such late hours, she occasionally fell asleep halfway through the pothi, but Baba always woke her. She would hear Him tell her, "Wake up!" (Aye, Ooth!), and she would be roused from sleep in order to resume her reading.

One night, it was around 11 p.m. and Aai had lit a small kerosene lantern. A cotton mat covered the window under which she had placed the light. Soon, Aai finished reading the pothi, and fell asleep without turning the lantern off. A little while later, she heard a loud voice saying, "Wake up, wake up", and Aai woke up with a start.

To her fright, she saw that the lantern had fallen over with the breeze, and the cotton mat had caught fire. She immediately pulled the mat off and threw it out of the window. Then running to the kitchen, she was able to quickly bring water and extinguish the fire!

She knew that there were cotton pillows next to the lantern; and if she had not been woken by Baba, the room would have definitely been engulfed in flames in a matter of seconds.

Another such incident took place when Aai's son, Raju, who was a young boy then, lit few agarbattis and pushed them into a porous part of the wall near Baba's photograph. He always did this before going to play football, hoping that he would play well and win. That evening, in his haste, he quickly pushed the lit agarbattis and ran away.

A little while later, a man appeared at their doorstep and asked the children if he could see their mother. The children thought he must be confused and said that Masterjee was not at home. But the man insisted on meeting their mother and not Masterjee. Aai was in the verandah busy with her chores. The children came to her and said, "Aai, there is someone who insists that he wishes to talk to you and not to father."

Aai came to see what it was all about. Meanwhile, the man had stepped inside the house where he saw that some of the lit agarbattis had fallen on a bed sheet and it had caught fire. The man swiftly took the bed sheet and the burning agarbattis and threw them out. Seeing this, Aai brought water to quickly diffuse the fire. The man then told her that he had seen the fire starting and entered their house to intervene.

Aai thanked him and then asked, "Who are you and why do you wish to speak with me?"

"Oh no, I wanted to get an appointment to meet the man who reads people's fortunes", he said politely.

Aai told him Masterjee was not at home. Saying he would come the following day to meet Masterjee, the man left, never to be seen again!

According to Aai, it was nothing but Baba's intervention. He ensured the fire was doused before it went out of control. While narrating this incident, Aai said humorously, "If Baba did not save us, we would be crying to Baba that we lit agarbattis near Him and they caught fire. So to prevent our complaint, Baba Himself took care!"

ॐ

Baba bestows this kind of attention and love upon His devotees when they surrender to Him fully.

Aai's Vision Of A Break-In

Aai and Masterjee's home was being renovated, so for a few days, they had temporarily moved to another house close by. Their daughter's school board examinations were also taking place during this period.

Once, Aai was sitting in deep meditation with her eyes closed. In her meditative state, she saw that a man was at the window and was trying to open the cupboard from outside with a long stick, which had a sharp sickle attached to the end.

Aai immediately came out of meditation and entered the other room. To her horror, that was exactly the scene being played out. Aai could see a large man who had climbed up on the ledge outside the window and was trying to open the cupboard with a stick and a sharp sickle attached to it. There weren't any valuables in that cupboard except for her daughter's exam entrance card without which she would not be allowed to appear for her exams.

Aai spontaneously went to the window, grabbed the sickle and held onto it tightly. She says she did not know where she got the strength from but she tugged at the sickle and gripped it firmly.

The man was strong and Aai lost her grip, but in the process, he fell down from the ledge and tried to escape. Aai started shouting and raised an alarm. Bruised by his fall, he was caught by the neighbours who handed him to the police. It turned out that he was quite a notorious thief who had caused a lot of trouble in the neighbourhood.

Many people came to visit Aai and asked her how she had managed to overpower such a dreadful thief and throw him down. Aai did not feel it was her own doing at all and instead she attributed all of it to Baba, who would always oversee their welfare.

Masterjee's Father Passing Away

Aai and her family had once gone to Shirdi. On the way there, they also visited the Saptashrungi temple, which is about 60km away from Nashik. Masterjee's father was not keeping well at the time.

As they entered the temple, a woman suddenly approached Aai and prohibited her from entering, telling her, "Do not go inside, you are in mourning!"

Aai asked "Why? Mourning about what?"

The woman exclaimed, "Your father-in-law is dead!"

Aai spontaneously uttered these words to the woman, "No, he will die only after my husband meets him."

Deep within, Aai wondered why such a seemingly good woman would make such an ominous announcement. She prayed to Baba, wished the woman well, and proceeded to enter the temple for darshan.

A few days later, after their pilgrimage, they returned

home to Goa. At the door, there was a telegram waiting for them. It read, 'Father is seriously unwell, please come home immediately.' Masterjee was quite sad. The telegram was dated 19th of April and they had reached home on the 6th of May. He felt that by then, it was surely too late and his father had most probably passed away.

Aai at once told him, "No, he is alive, go to him immediately". So, that same day, Masterjee left for his family home in Jamkhandi by bus.

When he reached, to his great relief, his father was still alive. Masterjee met him and spent some time with him, after which his father declared, "I am going tomorrow!"

The next day, Masterjee's father passed away peacefully. Aai's prophetic words were once again fulfilled.

Masterjee sitting on the chair to the right with his parents as a child

Oil Cans And Baba's Generosity

One day, there wasn't sufficient oil at home for Baba's temple. So Aai asked Masterjee to get some from the market on his way home from work. This was during a period of severe financial stress. It was the fourth day of the month but Masterjee's salary had not come in yet.

Aai casually told Masterjee, "See, each time we depend on devotees to donate oil. This month let us spend some money and get it ourselves. If there is no money, see if you can get some oil on credit."

Masterjee went to one of the shops in the local market and asked the shopkeeper if he could get a large tin of oil on credit. The tin would cost around 300 rupees and Masterjee requested for credit until the end of the month. The shopkeeper agreed and wrote out a credit note. Masterjee gave him four annas as a token and took the tin home.

Upon reaching home, he taunted Aai, "See, I have brought the oil. I will have to pay 300 rupees for it!"

Aai did not like his tone and she asked him, "Why are you talking like this? You have not spent a paisa from your pocket all these years – neither for oil, nor for incense sticks or flowers – so why speak like this now?"

Masterjee quickly apologised, "Oh, I didn't mean it like that, please forgive me. But I do have to pay 300 rupees by the end of the month."

Aai said, "No, no, this is not all right, Baba will not like this! Having to pay 300 rupees is fine, but why make such a big fuss about it?"

Masterjee replied, "The 300 rupees will cut into our already small budget, won't it?"

Aai silenced Masterjee by saying, "Our budget is always tight, we are always hungry, always thirsty; our needs are never-ending. Somewhere we have to stop."

The next day, Masterjee went to work as usual. Strangely, at about 11.30 a.m., an elderly man riding on a Bullet motorbike and emanating a strong presence reached their home, asking for Masterjee.

He knocked on the door and asked Aai, "Where is the person who reads people's fortunes?"

"He has gone to school and will return at around 2 p.m.," Aai replied.

The visitor said to her, "No, no, he is coming now."

Aai was surprised to hear that and said, "How can he come now? School ends at 1.30 p.m. after which he will catch a bus and come home."

The old man once again repeated very confidently, "No, no, he will come now!"

It so happened that Masterjee came home early that day because exams were going on and the school day got over sooner than usual. Aai saw him walking back home from a distance.

The old man exclaimed to Aai, "See, here he is!"

As Masterjee entered the home, the old visitor introduced himself and sat down. Aai offered him some tea and just as they were about to discuss the purpose of his visit, the postman appeared with a telegram. It was a money order for 150 rupees from someone in Bihar (a state in east India) named Mr. Mishra.

The accompanying message said, 'This money is towards an offering for flowers and oil for Baba.' Masterjee had no clue about who this mysterious sender was but he tipped the postman, thanked him for delivering the money order, and resumed his talk with the old visitor.

Their guest said, "I would like to have my horoscope read but I am in a hurry to reach somewhere now. Can I come tomorrow?" Masterjee agreed to read his chart the next day and they fixed a time for the session.

As the old man was about to leave, he drew out a sealed envelope from his bag and gave it to Masterjee. He said, "This letter is from someone from Manali (a town in the northern state of Himachal Pradesh) who told me about you and asked me to hand it to you when we meet."

The old man bid them farewell and left. Masterjee was curious to read the letter and opened the envelope. To his great astonishment it did not contain a letter, but instead there was an amount of 700 rupees in it!

Taken aback, he showed the money to Aai, who gently admonished him, saying, "You spent 300 rupees and got back much more than that. Let us not make our hearts so small. What are we giving Him? We are only taking, for what can a child give its mother?"

ॐ

In my various meetings with Aai, I often noticed that she is very protective of Baba. She frequently tells devotees, "If there are faults in us, by all means, please point a finger at us, but do not ever say anything negative about Baba!"

The next story is a very touching incident; a true miracle of Baba that shows how He looks out for the welfare of His devotees.

Offering Food To The Old Man

For Aai and Masterjee, there were days in their life when even daily sustenance seemed difficult for their family. One afternoon, a simple meal of rice and fish curry was prepared. It was Aai's nature to always serve her family first, and only after everyone else had eaten, would she sit down for her meal. That day was no different; she assembled the little remainder of the food on her plate and was just about to eat when there was a knock on the door. At their gate was a very old man, quite frail and feeble, who pleaded, "I am hungry, all I ask for is a meal and nothing else."

When Aai saw him, she immediately offered him her plate of food, which was still untouched. Only she knew that this was all the food there was at home, cooked or uncooked, as they were completely out of rations.

The old man gratefully ate his meal, blessed them and left. The family asked Aai why she did that and she told them, "He is an old man. At his age, he would have not survived his hunger without food. I am much younger and can keep myself going with a glass of water instead."

It is easy to give and share with another when one has surplus, but most people find it difficult to do even that. However, to give away everything when one has nothing arises only from a space of love and recognition of true oneness with the other.

What took place later that afternoon was a true miracle: A Sai Baba devotee who was a frequent visitor to Aai and Baba's temple had a dream in which Baba appeared to her and said, "I am hungry, will you give me some food?"

The woman woke up with a start and relayed the dream to her husband who initially ridiculed her. She did not know how to interpret the dream and what she was supposed to do. Her only thought was to visit Aai with food and her husband agreed to go with her to Aai's house during the evening aarti.

The woman immediately left for the market to buy some provisions. She loaded her car to its maximum capacity with food grains, lentils, tea, sugar, spices, oil, etc., and in the evening, she and her husband drove to Aai's home with the rations. She narrated her dream and told Aai she brought her some food items for she did not know where else to go.

After taking Baba's darshan and attending the aarti, the woman and her husband left happily. After their departure,

Aai told her family, "See, one man's hunger is appeased and we are taken care of for three whole months!"

Aai cooking food for everyone

ॐ

Sai Baba has said, "If you give food to the hungry, and a place to rest to the needy, God's grace will always be upon you."

Every morning, there are many visitors to Aai's home who know that she always has something to give them: These visitors are birds, cows and squirrels. Even at Masterjee's office, animals and birds gather outside every morning and wait for his arrival.

A photograph of Masterjee feeding a cow that came to their home in Candolim every morning, just before he left for work

How Baba Came Home

In 1977, one night, Aai had a dream in which Baba told her, "Your elder brother-in-law is going to return home. Keep some oil in a thali and see his reflection in it before letting him enter." So Aai faithfully made sure there was oil for the lamp thenceforth.

Masterjee's elder brother, who was a little disturbed, had been missing for twelve years. The family was always concerned about his wellbeing and prayed for his return.

A week later, Aai had another vision in which she saw someone come home and give her something. She could not see what was being given to her.

Meanwhile, schools had reopened and Masterjee had resumed his teaching. The monsoon season was in its full glory. It was the 22nd of June and a typical overcast day, when that afternoon, a few cars drove up to their house. A man named Abhaji Pansekar and a group of Baba's devotees were outside.

Abhaji called out to Aai from outside, "Baba has come.

Bring the aarti and come." Aai wondered what this was all about and stepped outside. Abhaji took Aai and the family to show them Baba's statue that they had brought. He said to them, "We have brought a murthi of Sai Baba. It is supposed to be installed in the new temple at Kopravado, Calangute. The temple will be ready tomorrow for *murthi sthapna* (the sacred ritual of establishing an idol in a temple). We can keep the idol in your home until then and perform aarti here before it is placed in the new temple."

Everyone was quite delighted; they brought Baba's idol inside, placed it on a table in Masterjee's room and then performed the aarti. Quite by coincidence, Aai and Masterjee had gone to Mapusa just the previous day and purchased a plastic table and some chairs. Aai offered all the guests some prasad and tea after which they left.

Suddenly one of the children exclaimed loudly, "Baba, if You truly and really love us, then You will not go from this house!"

Aai corrected the child, "What are you saying? How can we manage to take care?" Bringing an idol home was a big responsibility – oil, incense sticks, flowers and food were offered everyday during the prayers, and since their financial condition was already weak, Aai was naturally concerned about the added expenses.

Early the next morning, the family waited for the same group of visitors to come and take Baba's idol to the temple. They grew anxious as the hours passed and nobody arrived.

Finally, just before noon, Abhaji Pansekar and a few devotees came home and spoke to Masterjee and Aai. "A problem has occurred at the temple. There has been an unfortunate incident with one of the trustees. We cannot take this idol now and install it there. We have collectively decided to let Baba's idol remain here."

Everyone was overjoyed. They quickly bought fresh flowers and arranged other items of worship for the aarti and Aai offered whatever food she had cooked to everyone.

Coincidentally, for the aarti that day, Aai had used the same oil that Baba had instructed her to keep aside for welcoming home a family member. Through her dream, Baba had symbolised that He was her family member who would return home to her soon!

Masterjee and Aai were initially a little worried about how they would manage the extra expenses for oil, flowers, fruit and other items for the daily *Naivedhyam* (offering to a Deity) of Baba, but from then on, people visited their home for Baba's darshan and helped with offerings. Over time, with the help of other devotees, the room was transformed into a small temple that was open to everyone.

The idol of Baba that came home to Aai

How the next story came to be part of this book is quite a miracle. As I was composing the previous story, I remembered that Masterjee had mentioned that the above incident was published in one of the issues of Sai Leela (a magazine compiling the experiences of Baba's devetoees). I wanted to cross-check some details, for both Masterjee and Aai are old and do find it difficult to recollect minute details of the important events in their lives.

Without much hope of finding what I was looking for, I randomly punched in some keywords in the Sai Leela section of the 'Sansthan' website but I did not manage to find the article in its archives. Browsing the web I landed on another website that had a collection of devotees' experiences with Baba.

A strange feeling made me click on two links from the hundreds of links listed, and to my surprise, the author's name was Prahlad Huryalkar, Masterjee's real name! It was the exact story I was searching for! The story in the second link was an anecdote that I had heard Aai relate, but I had forgotten about it. Somehow it was all orchestrated to come into this book to share Baba's miraculous leela!

Baba's Distribution Of Suffering

It was the year 1980 and the Diwali holidays had begun. A devotee name Sri Jai Rao, son-in-law of the late Kishor Sahu (a local devotee known by their family for years), started frequently visiting Masterjee and Aai. He used to attend the aarti sessions in the evening at Calangute before going back home to Vasco (a city in Goa around 40km away from Calangute).

One Friday evening, during the aarti, Aai had a vision of some incidents unfolding close to Baba's murthi. She saw that Jai Rao had fallen from his motorbike and his head was sprayed with a white powder of some kind. That same night, Baba appeared in her dream and said, "Your Rao has fallen down and broken his hand. Do not worry much, it was predestined, but I am distributing the quantum of suffering." Aai woke up with a start and narrated the strange dream to Masterjee. He told her that it was just a dream and she should not worry.

The following morning, Jai Rao visited them at home where he and Masterjee spoke on different subjects. As it was noon, he was invited to join them for lunch. A young man called Bhanudas Noti happened to come for Baba's darshan. "This is my neighbour Noti, who is a motorbike pilot," Aai told Rao, as she was serving them the meal. "Noti is a true devotee of Sai Baba, he always helps those who are in difficulty." Rao exchanged pleasantries with Noti, who left after taking darshan. After the evening aarti, Rao also left.

As Rao was leaving, Aai advised him to drive cautiously. Rao said, "Bai, I have experience riding a motorbike even in America. I am a seasoned driver. Your fears are baseless." But Aai told him, "Rao, nobody can escape destiny. However, devotion to God mitigates the intensity of pain and causes less suffering."

Rao said lightly, "I don't understand the philosophy of destiny. Nothing will happen to me. You will see me tomorrow perfectly safe." He reached Vasco safely that night. On Monday, he came to visit them as usual and had lunch with the family again. He then decided to go back to Vasco at 5.00 p.m. Aai insisted that he stay and return to Vasco the next day, but Rao said that he couldn't since his wife was waiting for him. He left Calangute at 5.10 p.m. and at 5.45 p.m. he dashed into a cyclist at a place called Agashi. The cyclist was carrying wheat flour.

The cycle was badly damaged, but the rider escaped unhurt. Rao fell face down and a lot of wheat flour was sprayed all over his body.

Rao's spectacles were shattered and the motorbike's lamp was damaged. He had also injured his left hand. A small crowd gathered at the scene of the accident where Rao was unable to get up. It so happened that at that very moment, Noti was going back from Vasco to Calangute. He saw the crowd on the road and slowed down, stopping his bike to see who was injured. Noti could not believe his eyes; it was the same gentleman, Rao, who had exchanged greetings with him in Aai's house two days earlier. Noti lifted Rao and took him to a doctor's clinic nearby. After arranging first aid, he took him to Vasco by hiring a taxi.

At the same moment when Rao fell down at Agashi, a big bee stung Aai on her finger and her hand started to swell. She said to Masterjee, "Rao has fallen down, and Baba has mitigated his suffering this way. Let us accept it." Soon after that, Noti arrived to inform Aai about Rao's accident.

The next day, Aai, Masterjee and Noti went to Vasco to meet Rao. While they were there he got a phone call from his close friend, Lucio Miranda, who was in Mumbai. Lucio told Rao that some goons attacked him near Strand Cinema and forcibly pulled off his wristwatch, causing an injury to his left hand. The incident took place on the same day and at the same time as Rao's accident.

ॐ

This incident is a profound reminder of our interconnectedness. It beautifully illustrates how closely we are all interrelated. Destiny is not absolute; we are brothers and sisters in the Sai family. We all have to share pleasure and pain without any complaint.

The next incident is again truly miraculous. It shows how Baba took care of Aai and the family when they were in Shirdi and the children were ill. Aai often says that Baba always gets everything done and never takes credit for anything. No one can guess what strings He pulls in order to take care of His devotees. Blessed is the devotee who has truly surrendered!

Fever At Lendibaug And Baba's Help

It was May in the year 1980. Masterjee had just started his astrology readings at the local hotel. One of his daughters told him that all of them wished to go to Shirdi. Due to his work and meetings, Masterjee could not accompany them, so they expressed interest in going by themselves.

Aai, the three girls and the housemaid packed their bags. Masterjee gave them money for their trip and they were off on their pilgrimage.

They reached Shirdi and stayed there for over a week. They had sufficient money and since schools were closed for the summer holidays, there were no time constraints. The children had a great time feasting on cold drinks, ice cream, and all kinds of street food. Unfortunately, this caused them to feel unwell and they soon fell ill with fever and bouts of nausea.

Aai was concerned about their health and wondered how she could cope best with the situation. The children were suffering and were unfit to travel. Aai had just enough money to cover their expenses for the trip, but not for the unexpected illness and the extended stay. She thought that she could call Masterjee and ask him to come to Shirdi or arrange to send them more money for the medical expenses. They were keen to return home and quite exhausted from the scorching heat of May.

Since the children were in her sole care – because the maid had fallen sick too – she could not leave them alone, and so, she walked to a telephone booth with the children to call Masterjee. Just as she was about to pick up the receiver, a strange old man hurried towards her, screaming, "What are you doing here, what are you doing here? Go! Go to Lendibaug (the garden adjacent to the Samadhi Mandir with trees planted by Baba Himself)."

He was very intimidating and Aai was confused and a little frightened; she could not decide what to do because the man was being rather persistent. He kept yelling at them, "Go to Lendibaug! Go to Lendibaug!" They were already disheartened and exhausted, and in that frame of mind, they walked towards the Lendibaug garden where they sat on a bench under a tree. The children were restless – one complaining about fever, one vomiting and another one hungry.

They continued sitting under the shade. An hour later, at around noon, one of the daughters began to feel a little better. Aai reassured the children that Masterjee would send them money or come to pick them up as soon as he heard from them. She was torn between the need to inform him and her reluctance to make him unduly worried.

Near the temple, there was a small hotel named Bhagyalaxmi Guest House. An old devotee of Baba who was a regular visitor to Shirdi for the past 30 or 40 years was staying there. While he rested in his room after an early lunch, he had a dream in which Baba said to him, "My people have come, they are not well; help them!"

Roused awake, he started walking to the *Chavdi* (the place next to Dwarkamayee, where Baba would rest on alternate nights) not knowing where he ought to go. He happened to go to the same telephone booth that Aai had visited earlier and was similarly confronted by the same old man who shouted in Hindi, "What are you doing here? Go to Lendibaug! Go to Lendibaug!"

It all seemed very bizarre and the old devotee could not understand what was going on. Following the stranger's instructions, he started walking towards Lendibaug where he spotted Aai and the children sitting on the bench: One child was moaning in pain and another one was vomiting. He then spoke to the little girl who seemed to be in better condition than her siblings, who told him their story.

He approached Aai and offered to help them by getting them a place to stay where they would be provided with food and clean drinking water. Aai was initially reluctant because although he seemed like a kind old man, she wondered how she could trust a complete stranger with her kids. However, he kept insisting on a chance to be of assistance to them and since the children did need rest and proper care, Aai accepted his help.

He then took them back to Bhagyalaxmi Guest House where he called for food, and also arranged for a doctor to come and attend to the children. He told them, "Baba has given me the opportunity to serve you, please stay here comfortably till you are completely fine. My cook is here with me; he will cook for you as well so that you do not eat anything from outside. Stay here comfortably and don't worry about anything; I will look after you."

After they settled in, he told Aai that as soon as the children were better, he would call Masterjee and inform him. With the proper care, the children's health soon improved and Masterjee was updated on their situation. Once the children recovered sufficiently, he put them on a train to Madgaon (a city in Goa 47km away from their home) from where Masterjee could pick them up.

They reached home safely thanks to the helpfulness of this man. Exactly a month later, this kind person came to Goa to visit them in their Calangute home. It was then that he narrated to Aai how Baba guided him through a dream to reach out to them. He did not know how to find them but was sent to Lendibaug by the old man.

A photograph of Aai near Gurusthan at Baba's temple in Shirdi (on the left)

Keeping One's Sole Focus On Baba

Once, when Aai and her family were in Shirdi at the Samadhi Mandir, her son, who was a young boy at the time, quickly ran up and went near Baba's idol before Aai could stop him.

Aai does not approve of anyone standing above Baba's samadhi because she feels it is disrespectful for devotees to stand atop Baba's resting place. This has always been her heartfelt sentiment.

As her son climbed up in excitement, the priest admonished the child by brusquely saying, "Hey, you are not supposed to do that! Get away from here!" He was quite rude to him.

Aai was upset by the priest's harsh conduct. She internally said to Baba, "What is this? We have come to You to see You, and we are insulted…"

As soon as that thought crossed her mind, Aai saw a photograph of Baba to her left. Baba spoke to her through the image and said, "What did you say? You have come to Me, not to meet the priest! Don't pay any attention to the priest. Pay attention only to Me!"

Aai was taken aback and her attention immediately returned to Baba. The next time Aai visited Shirdi, that particular photograph of Baba near the samadhi shrine was not there.

ॐ

This leela is an important one because one should never lose one's focus on Baba and get distracted or disturbed by people or events. There are numerous devotees who complain about the condition of Shirdi today and get involved in finger pointing, and this leela serves as an important reminder about where a true devotee's focus should be.

The Heart Operation And Baba's Warnings

Deepak Mehta was a close friend of Rao's and came from an affluent family. His family was also close to Aai and would visit her very often. They consulted with Aai before taking any major decisions and frequently came to ask her for blessings and guidance.

Deepak's brother-in-law had developed a heart condition and required surgery. They asked Aai what they ought to do.

Aai had a dream in which Baba said to her, "Ask them to have him operated on in America or else he will not survive the surgery."

Aai had a clear message for Deepak's family and she asked Rao to convey it. Rao went to Deepak's mother and told her, "Listen, Bai's intuition is extremely strong. You know I have just recovered from the scooter accident that she forewarned me about, though I did not listen. Take her word very seriously."

Deepak's family was very hesitant to take him to America for treatment. They were all in Goa and wanted to be with him during his surgery and subsequent recovery process. So they decided to have his operation in Mumbai and arranged for a renowned American surgeon to fly in for the surgery since they could afford it.

Aai told them once again that this was not going to work out well.

Ignoring Aai's words, they fixed a date for the surgery and went to Mumbai. As luck would have it, Baba kept sending them signs backing up Aai's words: The first time, the doctor could not come on the scheduled day and the surgery was postponed. The second time because of the volatile political situation in India the operation could not be arranged. Similarly, yet another incident postponed the surgery even further.

Aai saw these as clear warning signals from Baba that they should not proceed, but the family insisted. Finally, they went ahead with the operation, and Deepak's brother-in-law did not survive the surgery.

The family was in a state of shock and Deepak's mother regretted their decision. She came to Aai and repented for not having listened. She was quite worried about her widowed daughter and what would happen to her now. Aai reassured her that she would be all right. A few years later her daughter got remarried and settled down well.

If one reads the Sai Satcharita there are numerous incidents mentioned where people suffered when they did not listen to Baba's word. Aai also emphasises that when devotees pray and ask for guidance, they must follow the instruction with an unquestioning mind and complete faith, or else it is as good as insulting Baba.

In many cases, Aai would tell such devotees who would ask for guidance, but still had their own mind made up about what they wanted to do, that it was better that they did not ask for Baba's guidance and did what they wished for or wanted instead, and faced the consequences of their action as it was meant to be.

Aai also stated that out of the numerous devotees that met her over the years, she could count on her finger tips the number of sincere devotees that wanted only Baba's love and grace and did not care for worldly things. Those few people, she states, had true devotion. Baba would say, "I will give you what you want, until you want what I want to give you." i.e. Self Realisation.

Aai's One Good Saree And Her Plea To Baba

The financial condition of their family was not very good. Aai, by her nature, never asked anyone for anything and sacrificed all her wishes or desires, so that Masterjee would never feel any strain due to her.

Aai had only a few sarees out of which there was one new saree that she could wear for the aartis or any festival, while the other sarees were torn, frayed, and only fit to be worn indoors.

One evening, during the aarti, Aai's sole good saree happened to tear. In disappointment, she said to Baba, "You do not want me to wear my only decent saree. If You want me to remain this way, then I will remain so without problem." This was the only instance in her life that Aai ever complained or asked for anything.

The next morning, a tourist from California came home to take Baba's darshan. This lady had a dream in which Baba appeared to her and said, "I want sarees to wear."

Unable to interpret the dream, she immediately went to the Mapusa market. Being a foreigner, she did not know anything about sarees, and bought a dozen of them in the same colour. She then gave them to Aai and said, "Baba asked me to get these sarees."

Aai was completely overwhelmed with this experience; she went to Baba and started weeping with gratitude.

ॐ

Ironically, till this day, Aai has been gifted numerous yellow sarees by devotees. She laughs that she now has nearly a cupboard full of them, but she accepts all with love as she does not want to hurt the sentiment of any devotee who may present her with one. But till date, her simplicity and modesty are the same. She has a few sarees she wears and the rest find their place in the cupboard, reminding her of this incident.

The Greek Man's Passport: Lost And Found

Peter, a young man from Greece, was visiting Goa. He was on vacation and had somehow come to know that Masterjee was an astrologer. Becoming curious, he went to meet him.

When Peter entered Masterjee's home, he immediately noticed photographs of Sai Baba and some other deities and asked Masterjee who they were.

After Masterjee told him about Sai Baba and the other gods and goddesses, Peter brashly commented, "India is a funny land – so many people, so many Gods, it's strange."

He then asked Masterjee, "Why is Baba's statue particularly decorated?"

Masterjee replied, "We believe in this saint and revere him as the sum of all Gods. Whenever we are in distress of any kind, we have faith that He is our protector and will look after us. This is our firm conviction."

Peter then commented, "India is a land of superstition. It is full of blind faith and strange beliefs."

Masterjee was polite and understanding of his youthful ignorance, and courteously told him, "Things are as they are and we are all part of it."

Peter asked Masterjee to look at his chart and he agreed saying that he would work on it and give him a reading that he could collect in a few days. Peter then went back to Baga beach where he was staying.

Late that night, around 11 p.m., someone started knocking on Masterjee's door and he wondered who it was at that odd hour. He opened the door and to his surprise, it was Peter. He was shabbily dressed and looked scuffed up and troubled. Masterjee started to say, "I have not yet prepared your chart…"

He interrupted Masterjee and said, "No, no, I have not come for the chart. I have come to ask for your help!"

Masterjee paused and then offered, "What help can I provide you?" Peter went on to tell Masterjee that after meeting him, he returned to his room at Baga where in the evening he went swimming for a long time. When he returned to his room, he noticed that his wallet, passport, money, and some other important papers were missing. He told Masterjee that he was not worried about his money but about his passport. Masterjee asked him to go and inform the police first.

"I have already informed the police but they are unable to help me. This morning, you told me that Baba can help us in times of difficulty, so will He help me now? I cannot re-apply for a new passport because I have some judicial proceedings against me in Greece and I cannot approach the embassy." Peter also asked Masterjee to share his dilemma with Aai.

Aai assured Peter, "Yes, Baba will help you, provided you trust Him."

In the spur of the moment, Peter said, "Yes, yes, I will trust Him."

Aai asked, "What do you love the most, without which you would become absolutely restless?"

After some hesitation, Peter quietly confessed, "I have been using drugs and injections every few days for the past six or seven years. Without these, I get very restless."

Aai then told Peter, "Are you willing to sacrifice this in order to feel more calm?"

Peter said he was sorry that he didn't have money to offer them instead, but Aai was not interested. She said, "Baba is not a merchant here who has opened a shop. Give up all these injections and drugs. Are you prepared to sacrifice them?"

After contemplating for a few minutes, he agreed, though he did not quite know how it would help. He then pulled out his small bag of injections and bottles and was ready to surrender them. It was apparent that something within him had shifted.

Aai said to him, "You may go now. Baba will take complete care of you, and you will get your money and other items back. But remember, you should not consume any of these substances again."

Masterjee also casually reassured him, "Do not worry, you will find your valuables somewhere close."

When Peter went back, he stayed off drugs and started getting convulsions in the next few days, seeing which his friends admitted him to a hospital. Surprisingly, he was determined not to use any narcotics again, and with firm resolve and full faith in Baba, he stayed off drugs.

A month later, he came back to visit Masterjee and Aai and asked them about his wallet which was still missing. Masterjee spoke to Aai and then relayed her message to Peter, "Have faith in Baba, and you will find it somewhere in the vicinity of your home. Don't worry, it will come to you."

A few days later, Peter came to their home and he was visibly moved. A miracle had occurred: There was excitement in his voice and tears in his eyes as he spoke, "See! My bag, passport, money and papers – exactly as they were! It was all buried in the garden behind the room. This morning, I noticed a dog digging some earth and I saw a small packet hidden in the soil and pulled it out. It is slightly damp, but all the contents are intact!"

He was so thrilled and excited that he said to Aai, "How much money do you want? I wish to offer some!"

Aai refused, politely saying, "No, we have not opened a shop for Baba here. However, if you feel like, you can distribute some sweets to the children who play at the football ground here."

The next day, an excited Peter came to the family with a car full of goodies. He had brought cakes, breads, sweets, chocolates and even fresh eggs, all of which he gave as an offering in front of Baba's murthi. Aai was not home that morning and when she returned, she was startled to see raw eggs placed before Baba. She sent for Peter and asked him to distribute it among the children who were playing outside at the football ground.

After this, Peter went and narrated the incident to the police. He meant to withdraw his complaint about his missing valuables, but they got suspicious about how Masterjee knew the whereabouts of his lost wallet. They told him that Masterjee was probably the culprit! Peter ignored them and cancelled the complaint.

After a few months, Peter's father came to see Masterjee, and although he could not speak English, he somehow managed to communicate, "Our son had been on drugs for the past six years. We've tried everything to make him stop, but it was impossible. And now it has happened as a miracle!'

Aai later told Masterjee that it was Peter's faith, complete surrender and trust that was the real miracle!

ॐ

When I spoke to Aai about this incident, she clearly said that it is each one's faith and devotion that counts; it's really not her doing at all. What a beautiful miracle it was that once more reaffirms our absolute faith in Sai, the protector of all.

Aai advises us to see Baba as our mother – have complete trust in Baba like a child has in its mother. Once Baba takes care of you, there will be nothing to worry about.

The Story Of The Lost Earring

One morning, as Masterjee walked to school, an old woman in the neighbourhood called out to him rather frantically, "Masterjee, Masterjee!"

The woman was a coconut seller who could just about manage to make ends meet. Over the past few years, she had saved some money to buy a pair of gold earrings and that morning, she happened to misplace one of them. After searching in all the likely places, she was still unable to find it and was naturally anxious.

This woman knew about Aai and the miracles that had come to be. So when she saw Masterjee, she called out to him to ask if she would ever find her lost earring. Masterjee was in a hurry to get to school on time and casually told her that she would definitely find her earring. The woman wanted to know details as to when and how she would locate it, but Masterjee left after reassuring her that she would surely find it.

Not satisfied with his reply, the woman went to their

home to meet Aai. There, she narrated the incident to her and asked for her opinion.

"What did Masterjee have to say?" asked Aai.

"Masterjee has assured me that I will surely find the missing jewellery", said the woman.

Aai said simply, "If he has said so, it will happen. Have faith and patience."

The woman was restless and kept asking Aai for details, but Aai simply repeated that she should have faith in Baba and would get her earring back as Masterjee had told her.

After hearing Aai's words, the old woman's confidence was restored and she went home. She proceeded to tell her neighbours about the incident and the reassurance she had obtained from Aai and Masterjee. Most of them discouraged her, saying that a tiny little earring would never be located.

The old lady kept searching and talking about the missing earring. Months passed and there was still no sign of it. Her neighbours mocked her and suggested she give up all hope.

Once again, she went to meet Aai, who reassured her by saying, "I do not know how or when, but you will find it, so be patient and have faith."

A year and a half passed; the incident had blurred in the woman's memory by then. It was the season to pick coconuts and she was occupied in the plantations.

One morning, as she was working in the plantation behind Aai's verandah, she stepped on a sharp object and experienced shooting pain. Thinking it would be a shard of glass or a rusty nail, she bent down to dislodge it and to her amazement, it was the missing earring!

It was a miracle that the tiny object was found. What were the odds of finding a small object by the same person who had dropped it a year and a half ago, in an area where there was a lot of footfall?

It is a coincidence beyond the scope of rational thinking. The old woman was simple overjoyed. She rushed to thank Masterjee and Aai and as the news of this incident spread, the villagers were equally amazed.

Masterjee doing an astrology reading

There are numerous instances where Saints such as Sai Baba or Swami Samarth, would perform leelas so that the word of their devotees would come true. This leela illustrates this. Aai says a pre-condition for this is that one must be completely truthful and honest as a devotee.

The next leela is even more incredible! While searching for the picture of Baba that had been eaten by white ants (mentioned in a previous story), an old handwritten letter fell out from the cardboard backing while we were trying to get the photograph out. It is an account of a devotee's miraculous experience of Baba in the past. Masterjee could remember this person but had completely forgotten about the incident until then. Over the years, many miraculous incidents took place, but this one truly is a special tale that came to us in a unique way. It is presented in the next chapter.

The Invisible Bus Conductor

It was the year 1984 and the auspicious day of Anant Chaturthi. There was the customary aarti at Aai's home in the evening and many devotees had gathered, including a regular visitor named Narayan who ran a local bus service between Panjim and Calangute. He was an ardent devotee of Baba and had deep faith in Him.

That evening, during the aarti, Narayan sang with abandon as he always did. After the aarti was over and prasad had been distributed, people took blessings of Baba and began to disperse. Narayan was casually chatting with Masterjee when, suddenly, Aai approached him and asked, "Narayan, where is your bus? Today Baba's expression is that of concern." Narayan immediately looked at Baba's murthi and also got the same feeling of unease.

A few minutes later, a man came running to their home urgently looking for Narayan. He seemed quite flustered. On spotting him, he said, "Some troublemaking passengers got into a brawl with the conductor and there was a big scuffle. We have parked the vehicle near the bus stand by the sea face. Come with me immediately. Those same people are now on the lookout for the bus when it returns; as we go past Candolim, they'll be waiting for us."

Narayan quickly took Aai and Baba's blessings and left to mediate and help in pacifying the situation. He boarded the bus with both the driver and the conductor.

Since it was an auspicious day, there were a lot of people who had gathered by the sea for the submersion of Ganesh idols. The bus had to move slowly; people got on and off the bus, but there was no trouble.

They managed to safely reach Panjim from Calangute. However, on their way back to Calangute, they were stopped at Candolim by a throng of people who were angry about the earlier incident and on the lookout for the conductor. They were going to beat him up. (It is not clearly mentioned in the handwritten note what exactly the brawl was about, but apparently it was something serious.)

They quickly put large stones around the bus so it could not move further. An angry mob surrounded the bus and started looking for the conductor. Narayan intervened and asked them, "What happened? Please tell me."

Tempers were high and the angry crowd was in no mood to talk or be rational. They were screaming and shouting, and started rattling the bus in an attempt to get inside.

The irate mob shrieked, "Where is that dammed conductor? Bring him before us now!"

Narayan was frightened for his own life as the fear of violence breaking out was very real. He knew that those people wanted to attack him and kill the conductor. He felt responsible for the man because it was his employee. He sent a silent, heartfelt prayer to Sai Baba, "Baba, only You can save us now!"

More people joined the angry mob; there were more than 25 people by then. They forced open the door and entered the bus, going straight to the driver's cabin where Narayan, the driver, and the conductor were all present. They started screaming and asking, "Where is the conductor?" Narayan did not say a word; he was trembling in silence.

What happened was truly Baba's miracle. The conductor who was right behind Narayan became invisible to the mob! 25 pairs of eyes were searching for the man and no one saw him, although he was cowering behind Narayan the entire time.

The mob inspected the bus, looked all around but could not find him!

Narayan understood this was Baba's divine play. Some people from the throng got off the bus and another lot of people got in, but they couldn't see the conductor either!

"Baba is indeed a divine magician!" Narayan exclaimed in his heart. Judging by the mob's mood, they would have most certainly not left the conductor alive, and would probably have burnt the bus down as well. After the enraged crowd left, Narayan quickly drove to the police station and registered a formal complaint. He then came back to Baba's temple and fell at His feet!

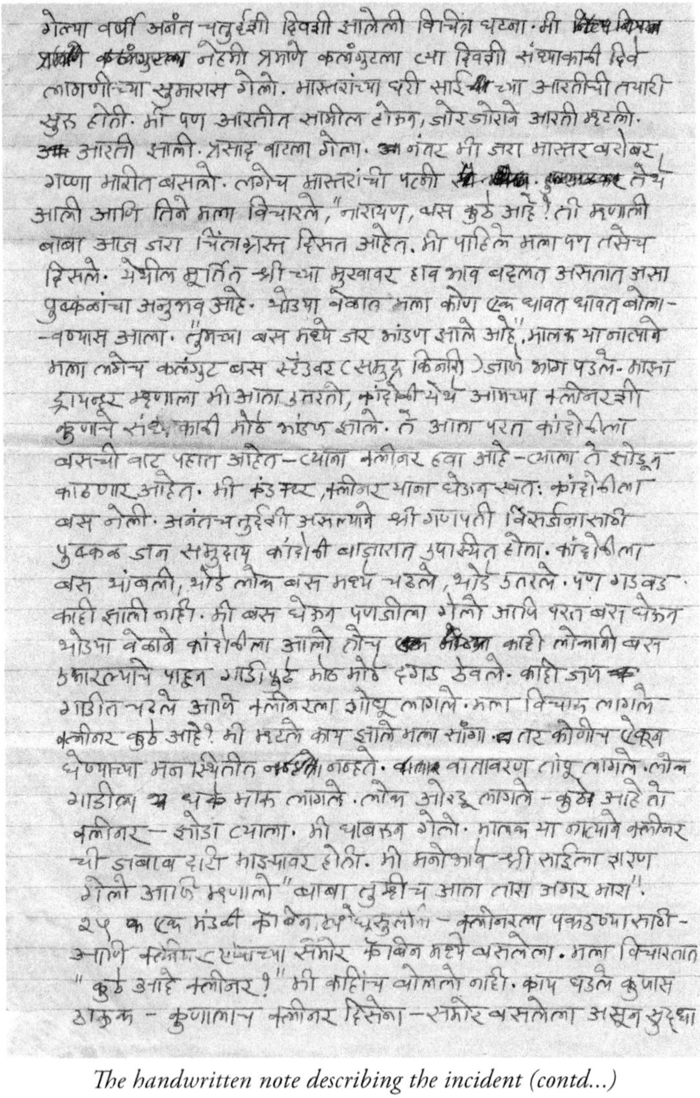
गेल्या वर्षी अनंत चतुर्दशी दिवशी आलेली विचित्र घटना. मी नेहमी प्रमाणे कलंगुटला त्या दिवशी संध्याकाळी दिवे लागणीच्या सुमारास गेलो. मास्तरांच्या घरी साईच्या आरतीची तयारी सुरु होती. मी पण आरतीत सामील होऊन, जोरजोराने आरती म्हटली. आरती झाली. प्रसाद वाटला गेला. नंतर मी जरा मास्तर बरोबर, गप्पा मारीत बसलो. लगेच मास्तरांची पत्नी तेथे आली आणि तिने मला विचारले, "नारायण, बस कुठे आहे? ती म्हणाली बाबा आज जरा चिंताग्रस्त दिसत आहेत. मी पाहिले मला पण तसेच दिसले. येथील मूर्तित श्री च्या मुखावर हाव भाव बदलत असतात असा पुष्कळांचा अनुभव आहे. थोड्या वेळात मला कोण एक धावत धावत बोलावण्यास आला. "तुमच्या बस मध्ये जर भांडण झाले आहे", मालक या नात्याने मला लगेच कलंगुट बस स्टँडवर (समुद्र किनारी) जाणे भाग पडेल. माझा ड्रायव्हर म्हणाला मी आता उतरतो, कांदोळी येथे आमच्या क्लीनरशी कुणाचे संध्याकाळी मोठे भांडण झाले. ते आता परत कांदोळीला बसची वाट पहात आहेत - त्यांना क्लीनर हवा आहे - त्याला ते झोडून काढणार आहेत. मी कंडक्टर, क्लीनर याना घेऊन स्वतः कांदोळीला बस नेली. अनंतचतुर्दशी असल्याने श्री गणपती विसर्जनासाठी पुष्कळ जन समुदाय कांदोळी बाजारात उपस्थित होता. कांदोळीला बस थांबली, थोडे लोक बस मध्ये चढले, थोडे उतरले. पण गडबड काही झाली नाही. मी बस घेऊन पणजीला गेलो आणि परत बस घेऊन थोड्या वेळाने कांदोळीला आलो तोच काही लोकांनी बस थांबल्याचे पाहून गाडीपुढे मोठ मोठे दगड ठेवले. काही जण गाडीत चढले आणि क्लीनरला शोधू लागले. मला विचारू लागले क्लीनर कुठे आहे? मी म्हटले काय झाले मला सांगा तर कोणीच ऐकून घेण्याच्या मन स्थितीत नव्हते. वातावरण तापू लागले. लोक गाडीला धक्के मारू लागले. लोक ओरडू लागले - कुठे आहे तो क्लीनर - झोडा त्याला. मी घाबरुन गेलो. मालक या नात्याने क्लीनरची जबाबदारी माझ्यावर होती. मी मनोभावे श्री साईला शरण गेलो आणि म्हणालो "बाबा तुम्हीच आता तारा अगर मारा".
२५ एक मंडळी कॅबिन, टपधरुन - क्लीनरला पकडण्यासाठी - आणि क्लीनर त्यांच्या समोर कॅबिन मध्ये बसलेला. मला विचारतात "कुठे आहे क्लीनर?" मी काहीच बोललो नाही. काय घडले कुणास ठाऊक - कुणालाच क्लीनर दिसेना - समोर बसलेला असून सुद्धा

The handwritten note describing the incident (contd...)

...contd. from previous page

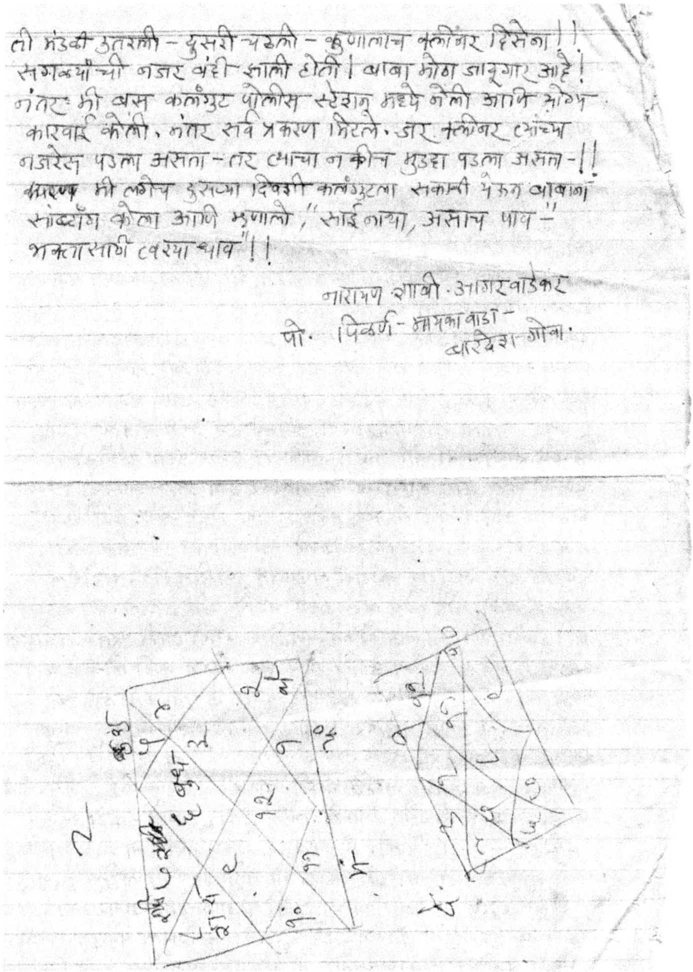

ती मंडळी उतरली – दुसरी चढली – कुणालाच क्लीनर दिसेना ! !
सगळ्यांची नजर बंदी झाली होती । बाबा मोठा जादूगार आहे !
नंतर मी बस कलंगुट पोलीस स्टेशन मध्ये नेली आणि योग्य
कारवाई केली. नंतर सर्व प्रकरण मिटले. जर क्लीनर त्यांच्या
नजरेस पडला असता – तर त्याचा न कोण मुडदा पडला असता – ! !
~~[illegible]~~ मी लगेच दुसऱ्या दिवशी कलंगुटला सकाळी येऊन बाबांना
साष्टांग केला आणि म्हणालो, "साईनाथा, असाच पाव –
भक्तासाठी त्वरया धाव" ! !

नारायण शास्त्री · आगरवाडेकर
पो. पिळर्ण – मायकावाडा –
बारदेश – गोवा.

A Desire To Meet Someone Close To Baba

On one of Aai's pilgrimages to Shirdi, when Aai had gone only with the children, she was sitting outside the temple one morning and thought that she desired to meet someone who was very close to Baba.

It so happened that about ten minutes later, a young woman dressed in a beautiful saree and gold ornaments approached Aai and requested her, "Please come with your children, I would like to get them something to drink."

Aai was a little hesitant to accept her offer but the woman respectfully insisted.

People around her were staring at the woman and she seemed to be quite well known. Aai and the children accompanied her to her house, which was large and not too far from the temple, where the woman served them flavoured hot milk.

Later, Aai was told that the woman was the daughter-in-law of Tatya Kote Patil, who along with Mahlsapati, were two of the most intimate devotees of Baba who were even allowed to sleep at the mosque with him. Aai then immediately understood the significance of how close the family was to Baba and was overwhelmed at how quickly Baba had granted her simple wish.

ॐ

Aai constantly says that complete faith in Baba and the will to surrender to Him enhance our personal experience. "Trust Baba as a child would trust its mother, see Baba as a child would see its mother, and you will be blessed by His grace, love and care," says Aai.

Many times, people ask her about her experiences. To this, she simply says that she really does not do anything at all. It is faith and trust in Baba that makes it all possible.

The Karma Of Money

Many years ago, a high-level minister came to Masterjee for an astrological reading. After the reading, she asked both Aai and Masterjee for guidance as she was going through some personal strife. After discussing her troubles with them, she felt very pleased and reassured.

Suddenly, the woman drew out a large bundle of notes amounting to 10,000 rupees and handed it to Aai. Masterjee's salary at the time was 120 rupees a month, so 10,000 rupees was like winning a bumper lottery. Masterjee was naturally thrilled.

Aai said to the woman, "We appreciate the sentiments behind this large amount but cannot accept it."

She gave the money back to the woman who reluctantly took it. She then thanked them and left.

Masterjee was quite upset and began to argue with Aai. "It was 10,000 rupees! We are short of money, how could you just return that amount?"

Aai told him very firmly, "Are you going to sell yourself for that sum of money? Do not ever do that!"

Masterjee said, "When you are willing to accept 20 rupees from the other locals, why not accept 10,000?"

"20 rupees is much more powerful than 10,000. You do not know the karma of that money. Every rupee has a different force depending on how the money is procured, from whom and for what work. Money that is earned truthfully, without any deceit or by harming someone will have a different, more positive force than money earned by depriving someone else of what is rightly theirs. It may look the same to you but it is not like that at all", Aai replied.

Although Masterjee was disappointed, he understood exactly what Aai meant. Aai was like Baba – very particular about her accounts. Once, she even insisted on cancelling her travel in order to return two rupees to a shopkeeper.

ॐ

Sai Baba would often say that 'Poverty is more precious than kingship' and Aai's life has embraced simplicity and contentment. There were numerous instances like this where, if she wished, she could have easily accepted many such gifts, but she never did. Another incredible trait of Aai's is that she looks upon one and all as equal, and there is no difference in her approach to one that is simple or one that may be decked with worldly fortunes.

Forewarning To An Accident

It was November of 1988. Some of Baba's devotees, a group of boys who ran a garage at Mapusa, came home to visit Aai and Masterjee.

One of them, Dayanand, had bought a new Ambassador car. They were very excited and had driven it to Aai's home. They had made a plan for Shirdi and wanted to invite Masterjee and Aai to accompany them too. Masterjee was free as he had three weeks off from school but Aai decided not to join them because she had to take care of the children.

They asked Aai for permission to go on this pilgrimage and she gave her consent. It was decided that they would come to pick up Masterjee by 3 a.m. since they hoped to have an early start and reach Shirdi by late evening.

The car arrived at their home. There were nine people in the group, including a young three-month-old child and Aai offered them tea before they began their journey.

As they were leaving, Aai came out and said to Dayanand, "You can certainly go on this trip, but heed my advice: after sunset or by 7 p.m. at the latest, do not drive the car. Keep this in mind. Go wherever you want, but I am only asking you not to drive after sunset. Stop wherever you are after sunset."

"Why do you say so, Aai?" asked Dayanand.

Aai said, "Just do it, because there is an indication of an accident. Do not drive after 7 p.m. Wherever you are, halt, spend the night there, and then continue the next morning." Aai was very assertive.

The boys heard her, but without paying much attention they left. They were very excited about their trip and took turns driving. They reached Shirdi safely that evening.

There, they took Baba's darshan and travelled to several nearby places of pilgrimage. Finally, they went to Trimbhakeshwar (a Hindu temple near Nashik), before returning to Goa.

On their way back, the route took them past some villages where the women in the group wanted to buy some local varieties of vegetables that weren't available in Goa. Since they were inexpensive, they wound up purchasing about 60 kilos of vegetables in all, which was packed and securely mounted atop the car's carrier.

Continuing their journey, they reached Pune city at around 5.30 p.m. Masterjee asked the others their plan for the rest of the evening. Soon, it would be dusk and he was aware of what Aai had said.

The boys said that Kolhapur (a city in Maharashtra 233km away from Pune) was not too far away and since the weather was quite pleasant, they would continue driving. Masterjee reminded them that it would be past 7.30 p.m. and Aai had warned them against driving after sunset. They brushed the topic aside and told him not to worry. Masterjee was not comfortable but didn't say anything since the majority had decided to go ahead.

They went to a restaurant on the outskirts of Pune where they all had a nice meal. Masterjee pointed out to Dayanand once again, "We can book a room here and spend the night, and then continue tomorrow morning."

Dayanand replied, "No, no, why should we stay here? We have bought a lot of vegetables that will get spoilt. Let us continue our journey. It's a new car, Masterjee, don't worry." Masterjee retorted, "These vegetables are going to create a problem for us." Nobody paid any attention to him, and they resumed their journey. At exactly 8.30 p.m., they were at the Katraj Ghat (a mountain pass around 14km away from Pune city). Masterjee repeated once more, "Aai had said not to drive at night", to which Dayanand replied, "Oh no, these women and their fears… we are all experienced drivers!"

After about 30km, the car suddenly stopped. Masterjee saw this as a warning sign, and put forth his suggestion once again, but they still did not listen to him. The boys were mechanics by profession and fixed the car in no time.

They went past a large tunnel and were now on their way to Kolhapur when the car stopped once again. Masterjee repeated, "This is an omen that something is wrong." Yet again, they brushed him aside and said, "Oh, it's a new car, sometimes these problems happen. Don't be paranoid. The petrol must be adulterated."

Being mechanics, they somehow got the vehicle moving again. It was now almost 1 a.m. Some people were chatting and cracking jokes while the others were fast asleep. Soon they reached Wathar junction, which was about 140km from Kolhapur.

All of a sudden a huge truck crossed them at an intersection and rammed into their car from behind! Within a fraction of a second, their vehicle was tossed to the side of the road and got badly damaged. A few of them were thrown out of the car due to the impact.

It was pitch dark and deathly silent. The truck did not stop but instead drove away. Everyone passed out from the impact of the collision. About 15 minutes later, Masterjee was the first one to regain consciousness. He lay on the ground and saw the car a little distance away: It was completely crushed.

No one else seemed to be conscious and he thought that they were all dead. He slowly got up, tried to walk, and with great effort, he reached the road. He tried to stop a passing vehicle to ask for help, but in vain. About half an hour later, a truck pulled over.

The truck driver directed the headlights at the spot where the accident took place. Masterjee could see his friends as they lay unconscious in and around the car. They were slowly stirring and coming round. It was freezing cold. They took stock of the situation – no one was badly injured except for some minor cuts and bruises. They found the child safe inside the trunk of the car, protected by parts that were badly crushed.

The highway police soon arrived and made their enquiries and reports. That night, while this mishap occurred, Aai had a dream in which she saw the whole room full of Baba's udi. She experienced a very strong smell of petrol. She intuitively realised that they had a collision and told the children in the morning that the group had not listened to her warning and had surely met with an accident.

When they reached home after two days, the boys were so embarrassed that they could not even show their face to Aai.

ॐ

In this Leela, it was Baba's guidance that had come through Aai and was ignored by the group.

There are numerous incidents in the Sai Satcharita where Baba would give advice to devotees, and those who did not pay heed to Baba's words faced many calamities and misfortunes.

Asking Baba For A Television Set

One day, the children said they wanted a television set at home. Feeling this may be a passing fancy of the children, Aai casually said to them, "Ask Baba and all your desires will be fulfilled."

The next day, Aai had a dream in which Baba said to her, "Mala bhiksha midali nahi", which translates to 'I did not receive it in alms.'

Three days later, Aai had another dream in which Baba said, "I have received a television set in bhiksha and will send it to you."

The following day, they had an unexpected visitor from Mumbai who brought a TV set as a gift! Aai was moved to tears.

She told Masterjee and the children that, henceforth, they should not ask Baba for worldly things and bother Him with such banal requests. She was overwhelmed by the intensity of Baba's love and care.

Resolving A Union Strike

On 15th December 1993, there was a flash strike at the hotel Masterjee was working at. It was a bad time for the hotel, as it was peak season and the workers' union went on strike.

The months of December and January passed, and the issue was not resolved. In fact, it was worsening, for the company was making losses due to zero occupancy at the hotel. Even the intervention of various influential people including the Chief Minister, various MLAs and the company's directors seemed futile.

One day, frustrated with the state of affairs, the General Manager came to Masterjee and told him, "Masterjee, please do something!"

"What can I do?" asked Masterjee, "I can only draw a horoscope and read astrological charts."

The manager knew about Aai and asked if he could come to their home and meet her. Aai agreed to see him.

She told him, "I will help settle the strike. Give it a few days. Things will work out."

Masterjee was puzzled. He asked Aai, "What is it that you are going to do?"

Pointing towards Baba, Aai replied, "I will not do anything. It is He who is sitting there, He will do it."

The next day, Aai instructed Masterjee, "When you go to work tomorrow, bring me one staff member who is part of the union, and that you know personally. Tell him that I have called him."

It so happened that one of the union members was Masterjee's former student. He came to Aai the next day.

Aai spoke to the young man, "This is a large company that you are dealing with. If you fight, you may win, but when? After many years: maybe 10, maybe 20. It is not a profitable fight. Consider your age now and think properly before you act. See that everything should settle down."

"I am willing to settle down, but what about the others? They are not willing to agree to the terms," the man replied.

Aai insisted, "Let them be. You think for yourself, and we will see what happens about the others."

The young man was part of the union's strike committee. He went back to the hotel and shared what had happened with his colleagues. Interestingly, another 20 came to see Aai the next day to air their grievances.

After hearing them, Aai told them, "See, you are fighting with a company that has unlimited resources. What do you have? You even have to pay for your own lawyer and now, your money is stuck because you are not working anymore. Think rationally."

Slowly, there was a shift in their thinking. In the next few days, the entire group of striking workers started visiting Aai. She then asked them to inform the company that they were ready for a dialogue.

Aai asked Masterjee to speak with the General Manager and ask for a meeting with the workers. She made it clear that she herself would not go to the hotel. So the next day, the General Manager and some other key people came to visit Aai. The main members of the union also came.

Both parties were sitting at opposite ends of the room. There was palpable tension in the air.

The General Manager was under stress. Aai put some of Baba's udi in his hand and asked him to keep it with him. The negotiations began and within about ten minutes, the matter was resolved amicably and the workers agreed to resume work.

News of the settlement reached Mumbai and other places, and a report was published in the newspaper too. People were amazed at the sudden resolution because it had been a long conflict, drawn out for several months.

Later, Masterjee asked Aai the secret to resolving this matter. Aai told him that everyone wants to be treated respectfully and lovingly. Once the workers' needs were addressed lovingly, people softened their stance and came to a harmonious agreement.

GOMANTAKTIMES

The man who saw tomorrow

This man succeeded where Calangute MLA Tomazinho Cardozo failed. He also predicted the murder of Rajiv Gandhi, but was ignored by everybody, including the press. ***EDUARDO RODRIGUES*** *on Masterjee.*

On 8 May 1991, in a non descript home in Calangute, a 61 year old man named Prahlad B Hulyalkar, more well known in Goa as Masterjee, scribbled through his rough pad the future of one of India's most visionary Prime Minister Rajiv Gandhi.

His prediction was that Rajiv Gandhi would not survive after the fourth week of May. Nobody believed him. Not even the press. So much so, that his prediction was not even published. What happened on that fateful week of May is now written in the history books of this country.

Yet, this man has no airs about himself.

Born in Jamkhandi a (State now called Bijapur) on 21 December 1930, Masterjee has seen ups and downs of life with sheer simplicity. The grandson of the last Chief Minister of the state of Jamkhandi before it merged to India, Masterjee settled in Goa in 1960.

Masterjee was a teacher and tutored in various schools until he retired as a teacher of St Theresa's High School, Candolim in 1991. However, from then on, he began to pursue his childhood hobby of astrology with renewed fervour.

Masterjee

Astrology, for Masterjee, is not a railway timetable. "It is connected with existence. "Astrology is a science of time in relation to individual existence. It does help us to prepare ourselves to accept and regret situations", is this man's summary of a hobby that he has been practising with great interest. Best of all, Masterjee charges no fees.

He views life through a spectrum of good and bad. And good to him is what is 'the least harm that is done unto others'.

Sex for him is "a biological need of a human being towards the one he committs himself and love is not restricted to only one".

And astrology is not his only hobby. Despite having an array of Indian as well as local politicians coming to him, Masterjee has always found time to help these in distress. He has intervened where our so called leaders have failed, and in the process has helped sustain many a family in terms of food, clothing and shelter. A case in point was the strike this year at one of Goa's premiere hotels -- the Fort Aguada. Tomazinho Cardozo, the Speaker of the Goa Legislative Assembly and MLA of Calangute failed to resolve the hotel strike despite the assurances to his electorate. After almost a month, Masterjee intervened. And by Jove! The strike was over "with no committments whatsoever to the striking employees.

"I used the human approach. You have to be genuine in what you are doing", is Masterjee's answer.

What does the future hold for our Prime Minister? Narasimha Rao will lose terribly he predicts. Not only will the Congress lose power at the Centre, but their chances that Prime Minister Narasimha Rao will lose his own Lok Sabha seat in the forthcoming parliamentary elections", is his prediction.

Coming down to Goa, Masterjee predicts that there will be a change in the Goa Government in 1996 and the same fate will befall most of the parties ruling in their respective states.

"The fall of N T Rama Rao is just the beginning of a very fluid political situation", says Masterjee.

Article in a newspaper about the Union Strike

ॐ

Baba did not like any conflict and arguments, and always asked people to avoid unnecessary disputes. Although this incident is fairly recent, it is hard to imagine that a simple pious housewife, revered for her saintly qualities, was able to bring about an amicable settlement between two warring factions of a large hotel chain.

Aai Knows One's Innermost Thoughts

When I first met Aai, I would visit her frequently, sometimes even daily.

We had a maid named Riya who was a devotee of Baba. Riya, a simple and pious woman of great dignity, was having trouble with her husband who was addicted to alcohol and did not take responsibility for her or the children. She had heard us discuss Aai at home and one day, she hesitantly asked if she could come and meet her.

I assumed she would like to discuss her domestic situation with Aai and seek her blessings and guidance, so I agreed to take her there on my next visit.

It was strange how events unfolded. I introduced Aai to Riya and the two of them started conversing in Konkani since they were both fluent in it.

Riya summarised her life with her husband and Aai was visibly angry. She told Riya that she needed to stand up for herself and that her husband needed to live by his responsibilities. After giving Riya firm guidance, Aai asked her to perform a particular ritual and fast every Thursday.

Aai specifically told Riya that on those days, she was not to think ill of anyone, curse anyone, or be malicious, for it would boomerang and happen to her instead.

In response to this, Riya told Aai that it wasn't her nature to curse or feel malice towards another. But Aai repeated herself and related an incident where she had suggested a similar ritual to another woman with the same warning, and it was unfortunately ignored.

Aai narrated that the woman, despite the warning, cursed another by wishing that she would be burnt alive. It so happened that she met with the same fate!

Hearing this account had a strong impact on Riya. She was visibly moved and I could see tears in her eyes. She then told Aai that there was something much deeper that had bothered her for many years that she never discussed with anyone – two of her sisters had committed suicide by setting themselves alight right in front of her eyes.

Riya said that although she had been trying to come to terms with the events, she hadn't really been able to. It was suppressed because suicide was considered a social taboo, and her family pushed it away and pretended it hadn't happened. But at some level, it affected their daily lives. There was a lot of anger, regret, guilt and fear because they did not know how to deal with the situation.

Aai then explained to Riya that she should continue to have unconditional love for her sisters because they had not committed any crime and that they would always be her sisters even if they weren't physically with her any longer.

I could see a deep sense of peace in Riya after hearing Aai's words. She was amazed at Aai's all-pervasive knowingness and immediately sensed that Aai's narration of the incident was no mere coincidence.

A few months later, Riya's situation improved with her husband to the point where he asked her to stop fasting, saying that he would fast instead!

For some reason, Riya could not put off doing what Aai asked her do. This happened for two consecutive weeks and what happened next was another miracle. Riya had a dream in which she was visiting the Samadhi Mandir of Sai Baba where He said to her from His samadhi, "Continue to do what I have asked you to do every Thursday, it is good for you!"

ॐ

Oh how mysterious are the ways of the saints, how perfect their knowledge! How miraculous! How blessed she is!

May this story inspire the reader to have complete faith in Sai and surrender to Him.

This dream and story is also a reaffirmation of what Baba has said, "Have faith in Me. Even though I give up this body, My bones in My samadhi will give you hope and confidence. Not only I, but also My samadhi will speak, move and communicate with those who surrender to Me wholeheartedly. Do not feel disappointed that I am away from you. You will hear My bones speaking and discussing your welfare. If you remember Me constantly and have faith in Me then you shall be greatly benefitted."

Miraculous Settlement Of A Property Dispute

Aai was quite fond of a woman named Asha who was a devotee of Baba and a frequent visitor. She would give her some personal time during each of her visits. Sometimes, I happened to be at Aai's home when she came by and I witnessed the unfolding of a miraculous turn of events in Asha's life.

Asha used to tell Aai about a property dispute that had been bothering her. Ever since she could remember, her father and his sister were unable to see eye-to-eye regarding a disputed plot of land and their ancestral home.

Asha's grandfather had passed away without formally dividing the property between his two children. Asha's family was living in the ancestral house but the aunt claimed it to be solely hers, and she was further instigated by her husband and family. Asha's father was keen to end the mess by selling both assets, taking half the money and moving on. However, his sister was of a greedy and calculating disposition. She refused to cooperate with them and enjoyed creating trouble.

Soon, Asha's father passed away and Asha was thrown into the thick of things against her wishes. The cunning and conniving aunt passed her time by sending legal notices of all kinds to harass Asha and her mother. She always threatened to drag them to court. It was a very stressful time for her and she often had to take leave from work and go from one lawyer to another to seek legal counsel.

She was frustrated and felt there was no way out this muddle. She did not want Baba to do anything since she didn't like to ask Him for things, but found solace in confiding in Aai because she loved her and considered her a family elder.

Asha cited to Aai the harassment she faced on a daily basis, and feared she was approaching a nervous breakdown. One day, Asha and her mom received a lawyer's notice ordering them to vacate their home. On another occasion, their electricity supply was cut off.

Aai could see much more than what was going on. She told Asha that she should not underestimate her sly aunt, and that she should be careful of her malicious intent. Aai asked her to be patient; Baba would definitely help her.

Asha was not particularly hopeful because she did not see how anything could change. Her aunt was a formidable woman who wouldn't suddenly become solution-oriented.

Meanwhile, things worsened and the possibility of losing their home was real.

Some time later, Aai told Asha that she would ask her to do something specific when the time was right. Until then, she asked her to be patient and not antagonise her aunt in any way, but instead continue meeting her.

One morning, Aai made Masterjee call Asha in the morning to convey her message.

Masterjee called and told her, "There is a particular rare eclipse that is going to take place today afternoon between 3.30 p.m. and 4 p.m. My wife has asked you to do something at this time: She wants you to take some grains of rice and hold them in your mouth. Sit in meditation with your wish in mind during the period of the eclipse. Once the eclipse passes, take the grains of rice and store them very carefully. After they dry, take a few of them and throw them on your aunt's head. She will then be influenced by what you have in mind, and your dispute will be resolved."

Asha was busy at work and did not expect to hear from Masterjee at that hour. She was surprised to hear such detailed instructions. It sounded a bit strange to her, but she also knew that Aai, like Baba, sometimes asked devotees to do unusual things.

She left her office early and got home by 3 p.m. Placing her trust in Aai's words, she followed her instructions.

After she collected the grains of rice, she wondered how she would be able to put them on her aunt's head without arousing suspicion.

That same evening, under the pretext of delivering some mail, she visited her aunt. She sat next to her and managed to slyly do the needful. She then got back home and did not think too much about it. What happened thereafter was incredible!

In the past, Asha had suggested to her aunt that instead of selling both assets, one could take the home and the other the plot of land. This made sense to Asha but her aunt wanted everything for herself. She knew her aunt's ways only too well and highly doubted that she would agree to this proposal.

However, Asha felt motivated to try her best. She spoke with her aunt that night and persuaded her with this offer. She visited her the next morning to discuss this further. Surprisingly, the aunt agreed to the proposal on the condition that Asha and her mother vacate the house immediately after the exchange. She said she would go with them for the registration. Asha had been highly sceptical all along and could not believe her ears!

The following week, her aunt was leaving for Europe to visit her family. Asha was afraid that if there were a delay, her moody aunt would change her mind like she always did. It was time for immediate action. She quickly liquidated some funds and her friend's husband was kind enough to help her gather documents, visit a lawyer, and do the groundwork needed to complete this exchange. The process of getting the legal papers in order was humungous.

Asha called Aai and briefed her on what was happening and was warned not to sign any documents releasing her rights over the house until the plot was transferred to her.

Asha was in a state of disbelief but went with the flow of things. The lawyer got them an appointment for the simultaneous registration and they all went there to complete the formalities.

Baba's leela unfolded differently. The lawyer had managed to complete only one set of documents – the transferring of the plot to Asha and her mother. Asha anticipated a scene at the last minute, but her aunt quietly signed the documents without a fuss! Soon the registration of the deeds was complete. Asha was incredulous.

The paperwork to transfer the house to the aunt's name was not yet ready and they all agreed that Asha and her mother would do their bit upon the aunt's return.

Asha was in a daze. It had not completely sunk in that their family problems, pending for decades, were suddenly over! She called Aai and thanked her profusely, saying that for a woman like her aunt who hadn't trusted anyone, it was completely out of her character to do anything like this.

A few days later, her aunt called her, screaming that she didn't know how Asha managed to do something like this and fool her.

Asha then realised it was nothing but Baba's intervention!

She pacified her aunt, saying that upon her return from Europe, all formalities would be completed. Things eventually ended well and Asha and her mother moved to a small rented apartment until they were able to sell their plot of land and purchase a home.

Everyone who knew her aunt found it hard to believe that a woman like her would sign anything without first securing her own interests. When she said this to Aai, Aai simply laughed and had a mysterious twinkle in her eyes.

ॐ

Baba's ways are mysterious. This is yet another miracle of Baba's that I have been blessed to personally witness.

Baba's Blessings For Aai

Through a series of coincidences, I came to meet some of Baba's intimate devotees, one of them being Hema Teotia from Gurgaon, who everyone lovingly calls Hema Ma. When I went to meet her for the first time, there were some astonishing leelas of Baba that I experienced first-hand at her shrine.

One of the most sacred experiences Hema Ma has been blessed with by Baba, is that Baba manifests udi in her shrine every Thursday and Ma distributes this to numerous devotees who request for it. Many years ago, Aai had heard of this, and mentioned to her daughter in passing that it would be wonderful to receive some of that prasad of udi. In time, this wish was completely forgotten.

While recording the experiences of Hema Ma, she shared another miracle of Baba's grace: She would reverentially place the photographs of devotees sent to her in front of Baba and He would bless some of them with a manifestation of a tilak of chandan.

Upon hearing this, I was deeply touched by Baba's love and compassion for His devotees. I requested Ma if I could also leave a few photographs with her in the hope that Baba would bless them. Hema Ma graciously agreed, and I carried some photographs with me, including one of Aai, on my second visit.

By that time, Hema Ma had come to know about Aai by watching her videos, and she too felt a love and longing towards her. She said that Aai reminded her of her mother and she had a deep desire to meet her in person to embrace her. I requested Ma to give me some udi for Aai that she generously gave. Upon my return home to Goa, a few days later, Hema Ma also sent me the photograph of Aai that had been blessed by Baba at her shrine.

In my next meeting with Aai, I took the udi for her and told her about Hema Ma and the leelas that unfolded. Aai simply smiled and told me about how she had mentioned her desire to have some udi from Hema Ma's shrine and how Baba had fulfilled that wish!

Another touching leela of Baba took place in my third meeting with Hema Ma in the year 2020. Just before leaving her home, Hema Ma gave me a small shawl that she asked me to present to Aai. Hema Ma once again told me that she feels an unbounded love towards Aai, and is moved by her humility and complete surrender to Baba. She then narrated the wonderful leela of Baba's around the shawl, that unfolded quite literally!

A few days before we were scheduled to meet, Hema Ma had bought Aai a shawl and kept it in Baba's shrine after praying to Baba to bless it. The shawl was left overnight and sealed in a plastic bag. To her astonishment, the next morning, when she got up to perform Baba's aarti, the shawl was wrapped around Baba's idol!

Baba then told her (Baba communicates with Ma), that He had now blessed the shawl and she could present it to Aai. We were both overwhelmed by this leela and Baba's grace. Aai accepted the gift with folded hands and prayed to Baba with gratitude.

This incident was a profound reminder to me about how blessed Aai is, and all the grace that awaits us if we too can surrender to Baba like Aai has!

Aai's photograph that has been blessed by Baba in Hema Ma's shrine

Pointers From Aai

It has been many years since Aai's experiences were first documented. During this time, Baba has blessed us with the opportunity to film Aai and share these videos through the YouTube channel 'Sai Baba's Devotee Speaks'. In these talks, Aai has spoken about her life journey and experiences as well as given some pointers about how devotees can deepen their devotion to Baba, and directly experience His grace and presence in their lives.

In this special section, Aai gives guidance on some of the important aspects of one's spiritual life. Her guidance comes from first-hand experience and by being a living embodiment of true and complete surrender to Baba.

These precious pointers from Aai are compiled from all the personal meetings I had with her, transcripts of video recordings, and her answers to questions that devotees frequently ask her.

These points are segmented according to their topics for ease of the reader. It is recommended that one read these pointers slowly, contemplate on them and assimilate them in one's daily living as inspired by Aai's devotion and life journey.

Establish A Relationship With Baba

Baba's relationship with His devotees is like a child's relationship with his mother and father.

If a child suddenly remembers his mother, what will he do? He will cry asking, "Where is my mother?" and keep trying to look for her.

At this stage, if someone were to offer him something else as a distraction, the child would not feel satisfied. Only when he finds his mother, he will finally feel happy and at peace.

Aai says, "Baba is just like your mother. When you love Him, He will look after your complete wellbeing.

"This is one of the most important things in life – love Baba above all else. Whatever are your joys or sorrows, tell them to Baba just as a child goes and tells his mother everything.

"Sai Baba is the one who truly oversees our wellbeing in good and bad times. Whenever you are in trouble, He will immediately stand with you to protect you.

"When a mother hears her child cry, she comes running and embraces the child. Just like that, Baba embraces His devotees and protects them when they call out to Him."

For this, however, Aai says one must constantly chant His name and meditate on Him.

"Remember, Baba already knows what we truly need and we must trust that He will give it to us, the same way when the child is hungry, he knows that his mother will bring him food.

"Nothing else is required; this is the crux of it – we must cultivate this faith that Baba loves us like a mother loves her child, and depend on Him for everything. This devotion and path of loving Baba is a very simple path unlike the arduous paths of tapas, fasting or penance."

If Aai has something that she needs help with, she calls out to Baba with single-minded devotion. Aai's faith is absolute that Baba will do what is needed and right for her. Her trust is in Baba and whatever He wishes for her – she does not have her own wishes, demands, conditions or questions.

Remember, only if you are devoted to Him, He will look after you. One cannot expect His grace if one is not devoted to Him or has not surrendered to Him. If the child does not call out to the mother, how can the child expect her to come?

You must be constantly surrendered to Him. If the remembrance and devotion is constant, then feel rest assured that you would be looked after. He will come in any form and take away your sorrows.

If you have this type of bhakti, then Baba Himself will

appear before you. This is the kind of love you must have for God, then nothing else will be required.

Do Not Ask Baba For Anything

With all one's heart, one must yearn and call out to Baba like a child will call out to his mother. One's internal prayer should be such, "Baba, you are with me, looking over me, and that is all I want; nothing else." Wanting money, jewellery, house, land, relationships, etc. are worldly demands and not appropriate to ask of Him.

Remember, your wishes will be granted to you only if He wishes so, and not by your will, so you must never be disheartened. Whatever is destined for you, whatever is God's will, that will prevail and nothing else.

Baba has the total power to even give His devotees things that were otherwise not meant to come their way because of their destiny. The secret is to be completely free of desire and pray to Baba as guided above.

Do not keep asking Baba, "I want this" or "Give me that". Do not try to impose your own will. Nothing will come your way if you keep asking.

If one wants something, and whenever Baba fulfils it, He does it through some other form. Suddenly, some person may come and give you what you desired or do your work. Remember that the 'someone else' is none other than Baba operating through that person. It is Baba who infuses the desire in that person and your wish is subsequently fulfilled.

One's Devotion Is Tested

As Kabir's saying goes, *'Dukh mein simran, sab karen, Sukh mein kara na koi, sukh me simran jo kare, toh dukh kahe hoi'*. This means that everyone usually remembers God in their sorrows and forgets about Him when situations are good. But if people remembered God even in their good times, why would they have any sorrows?

As Aai stated earlier, once a devotee calls out to Baba and depends on Him for everything, He will come to their aid. However, Baba observes the devotee and their conduct after He has solved their problem. Do they still remember Him? Or do they forget about Him and their devotion when engrossed in a favourable situation?

If you are call out to Him only when you are in difficulty, then you do not have unconditional love towards Him. It is important to meditate on Him unceasingly. Irrespective of external situations, our devotion and remembrance must be continuous.

On Arrogance And Complaining

Aai cautions us to never be arrogant and think, "I am important, I have a lot of wealth and power." Never take even the slightest pride; always remember that it is Sai Baba who is the doer and that He has given you everything.

When difficulties come our way, we must not complain. Dedicate your whole life to His worship and devotion, and one day you will reach the ultimate goal: You will have the Divine vision.

The path is indeed difficult, but the one who is sincere and earnest will certainly reach the end.

Develop Steadfast Devotion

Aai has severe pain in her back, and walks about with great difficulty. "That is how life and old age is", Aai says. "Despite one's circumstances, our devotion must be steadfast."

New devotees often ask Aai, "You are suffering with a painful condition, why doesn't Baba cure it for you?"

Aai responds that everyone has to face the perils of old age and go through this difficult phase; Sai Baba Himself experienced it. He accepted His aches with grace and we must also learn from His example.

Humorously, Aai adds that even Baba would walk

crookedly with great difficulty – just as she does – and devotees would have to support Him on either side.

With this understanding, one must separate one's temporary conditions of life – that keep alternating between pleasant and unpleasant – and focus on God and our ultimate goal of liberation from the cycle of birth and death. This is truly what Baba wants to give us.

Some say, "God has not given me anything, so why should I pray?" That is not the right attitude according to Aai. You will be given what you need; you must continue your worship.

Truthfulness

Ramakrishna Dev would categorically say that Truthfulness is the penance of the Kaliyuga; with Truthfulness alone one can reach God. Aai lays further emphasis on this and is a shining example of it herself.

The only exception, Aai says, is that if by saying a lie, someone's life may be saved. Pujya Dharamdas Bapa would also emphasise that if one abides by the truth, and their words, actions and deeds are all in alignment, then what one says will come to pass.

There are numerous instances peppered throughout the book that illustrate this truth: Aai's word has always come to pass. One may say that it is Baba's word through her coming true and she is merely the instrument, but again, Baba operates through her only because she is an embodiment of humility, surrender, devotion and truth.

Don't Make A Show Of Devotion

There are many devotees who make a big show about their devotion outwardly, but it is a very different story inwardly.

For devotees who wish to have a small shrine of Baba at their home, Aai recommends that rather than having an idol, they should keep a little photograph of Baba there and worship Him with love and sincerity.

Not much paraphernalia is required and Baba Himself would say this. In fact, if devotees came to Him with articles of puja and they had been malicious to a person or any creature, He would throw out these articles and drive them out of Dwarkamayee. Baba did not like hypocrisy one bit.

For worshipping Baba, Aai recommends simply using turmeric and vermilion powder, lighting a *Pancharti* (a lamp with five wicks) and reciting His aarti daily – it is that simple. In the end, what really matters is one's bhav.

To illustrate this, Aai narrated a story from her childhood wherein she would go and collect wild flowers, string them together into a garland and put it on Baba's photograph that she would worship.

One day her mother objected to her collection of these random wild flowers because she thought it was too 'simple' an offering. Aai then asked her that wasn't God Himself the maker of the flowers? Her mother had no answer, and Aai continued picking them and lovingly offering them to Baba.

Aai insists that inner devotion and depth of feeling matter more than anything external one may perform. She also warns against the tendency of some devotees to make an outward show of their worship. A true devotee will always recognise another devotee; the need for external signs only stems from insecurity and the desire for recognition.

While travelling, Aai recommends that we carry a small photograph of Baba instead of His idol because there are chances that the idol may get damaged during the journey and this would not be appropriate.

Aai feels glad that Baba's name is spreading to millions of devotees across the globe. She considers herself nothing more than a tiny dot amongst all those millions. Being an embodiment of humility, she keeps saying that the slightest trace of pride is truly one's downfall.

Power Of Satsang

In the Sai Satcharita, in His own words, Baba gives an assurance to devotees, "The ones who lovingly sing My praises and life story as kirtans, I am forever behind them, in front of them and on all four sides.

"Whoever does My kirtan, to such a one, I shall give the wealth of happiness, perpetual peace and contentment, always. Have faith in this promise."

Aai lays particular emphasis on *Satsangat* (holy company), prayer and collective kirtan of Baba. Aai says that when devotees come together, the collective bhakti of the group is superior and that energy uplifts all the devotees present.

In the earlier years, there would be daily evening prayers and Baba's aarti at Aai's home that many local devotees would attend. She suggests that devotees visit Shirdi to attend the aarti at the local Sai temple and also arrange to have small kirtan and aartis in each other's homes by taking turns.

Regular Practice Of Sadhana

When she was younger, Aai would regularly practice meditation early in the morning before the day and household responsibilities had begun.

Now, in her old age, despite her shooting back pain, she regularly does her pothi readings from 9.30 a.m. to 12.30 p.m. without fail. She is completely oblivious to the outside world during this period.

For devotees, Aai recommends that they sit for dhyana meditation every morning between 5 a.m. and 6 a.m. She says that at first, one's mind may wander and one will not be able to concentrate, but over time, the concentration will gradually increase. Aai also says that our intuition increases with this practice, and soon, we will be able to see a preview of future events.

One important guideline Aai suggests is developing steadiness of posture. Initially, when one sits for five minutes and increases the time in dhyana meditation, Aai says it is imperative that devotees do not move their body at all, not even an inch, once they are seated comfortably. Ideally, one can sit in the lotus posture, or padmasana, but for those who find it difficult, they can also sit on a chair and follow the same instruction.

According to her, the body is nothing but a cage made of flesh and bone, and our soul is trapped inside it. Therefore, Aai says one has to awaken the spirit that is inside us by placing our attention within.

In the Sai Satcharita, in chapters 18 and 19, Baba gives Hemadpant specific instructions on 'Meditation' and 'How To Meditate On Baba And Attain Oneness With Him'. It is recommended that the devotee read these instructions carefully and repeatedly to get this sacred knowledge from Baba directly. If practiced correctly and sincerely, Aai says that Baba will come closer to you and fulfil all your worldly responsibilities.

The Power of Japa And Baba's Name

Along with the dhyana meditation, Aai recommends that one chant Baba's mantra 'Om Sai Ram' ceaselessly. One can practice this *naam smaran* (remembering the name of God) of Baba throughout the day silently, within one's heart, as one performs one's daily duties.

In the Sai Satcharita, Baba told His devotee Shama the power of chanting His name. Baba said, "The repeated chanting of 'Sai, Sai' will destroy all the sins of Kaliyuga. A mere prostration before Me is enough to destroy the past sins of speech and hearing."

The chanting has to be done internally in the mind. Since the mantra is not too long or complicated, one can easily be immersed in one's daily work and constantly be doing the Japa mentally. As a result, all of one's actions become an expression of devotion towards Baba and are surrendered to Him.

Aai illustrates the power of taking His name by the wonderful story of Lord Krishna and His devotee Arjun:

She said even when Arjun was fast asleep, he would keep chanting, "Krishna, Krishna." One day, Lord Krishna was pressing Arjun's feet. Seeing this, Narad muni came to Lord Krishna and said, "Here am I – such an ardent devotee of yours – I chant your name all day, and yet, you are here pressing Arjun's feet!"

Lord Krishna replied, "Come and place your ear over Arjun's skin and hear the sound that emanates from within."

When Narad muni bent down, he could hear the steady Japa of, "Krishna, Krishna, Krishna, Krishna..."

Now that is the kind of devotion one must have – our Japa has to be continuous and unbroken.

Be devoted to whichever deity you are fond of and worship that form. It need not only be Sai Baba. It could be Krishna, Shiva or anyone else; but worship Them with your heart and soul.

One day we all have to go to God: this is the ultimate goal. So we must forget all else and focus on nurturing ceaseless devotion. The purpose of Japa is only so that our faith is reinforced. Some method is required for the devotee to remember God and, for this, Japa is the easiest to do.

If one does not remember Him, never calls out to Him, how can a devotee expect Him to be with them? We must constantly take God's name, only then is He with us. If we are forgetful and immersed in worldly affairs, then how can we expect God's grace?

Therefore, Aai says we must regularly do our Japa and it is not as big a thing that it is made out to be. If a person is sitting in one place and in their mind keeps reciting 'Om Sai Ram', it is simple and enough. Over time this habit sets in and the mantra will become an automatic force driving us towards God. There is infinite power in Baba's naam smaran. The more we focus on Baba's name, the less time we will have to focus on our worldly desires and problems. When we commit ourselves to Him fully, He will take care of our whole world for us.

When you are thirsty, you drink water, don't you? Devotion is also like that, a kind of thirst. One should thirst for Naam or Jaap of Baba and quench that thirst with devotion. As we are more committed to the practice, by Baba's grace, He will bless us with our own experiences of Him and our faith will increase.

Remember, it is only by God's grace that one is blessed to take His name.

Service And Charity

Selfless Karma yoga and Bhakti yoga is the path prescribed by Baba for most devotees in the Satcharita. Having compassion for all is, in a way, the essence of Baba's teachings.

Baba even demonstrated His oneness with all beings by

getting wounded when a cat or dog was beaten and He felt their pain as His own. This is the highest demonstration of oneness or non duality with all beings.

Aai encourages one to help those in true need. However, she says that if we experience even the slightest amount of pride or a feeling that 'we' are helping others, then that is our downfall. This feeling is very subtle and one has to be watchful about this sense of pride.

The correct way to do anything charitable is anonymously – where when one hand gives and the other hand does not know.

Annadaan

Any guest at Aai's home is always offered food and water; from devotees to different species of animals such as birds, cows, dogs etc., no one is allowed to leave without being offered something to eat and drink.

Baba can come to us in any form – His true form may never be revealed to us. But we know that He is the inner dweller in the hearts of all beings, and so, we can serve Him in whoever we meet. Baba has said that those devotees that see Him in all beings are the ones most dear to Him.

Aai and Masterjee are living embodiments of this teaching. In this book, the chapter 'Offering Food To The Old Man' shows us how Aai, by her own shining example, lives this teaching with no excuse.

Aai also says that when one is offered food as prasad by someone, they should never refuse it because food is Brahma and denying it is the same as insulting God.

Millions of people across the globe struggle due to poverty and hunger. Aai said a true devotee of Baba would never waste food or indulge in excessive consumption because that is taking away from someone else's share in the world.

Contentment

Most of Aai's life (largely until her later years) was difficult with a very humble beginning and facing the challenges of losing her father at a young age. Financially they lost their inheritance after he passed away, and even after getting married, Masterjee's income just about managed to keep their household running.

In one of my meetings with Aai, she spoke about how contentment is everything. She recalled instances in her life where, every morning, they wondered how they would get four annas so that Masterjee could travel by bus to the school (which was quite far away) where he would teach at the time.

Then somehow, from somewhere, a person would come by for an astrology reading and leave the same amount before going, and each day would take care of itself. She expressed that despite how difficult those times were, they were happy, joyous and content, having full faith that whatever their needs were, they would be provided for.

Aai then went on to talk about how, nowadays, the world is immersed in consumerism and people's wants are endless. As a result they are discontented and miserable. Baba would say that 'Poverty is a thousand times more precious than kingship.'

Aai knows that it is not possible for the house-holder to renounce their duties and responsibilities and live like Baba did; but she says it is possible for them to live within their means, be righteous and live by the principles Baba taught us by His own example. This is the only way to experiencing peace and contentment.

Beware Of New-Age Gurus And Baba's Channels

Self-realisation or complete liberation is a very rare occurrence. In the Sai Satcharita, Hemadpant has written about this in much detail, where he forewarns devotees about those people who may display occult powers; they may be very learned, but rare indeed are true self-realised saints who are here only to uplift man.

In today's age, there are numerous pseudo gurus, teachers, guides, and channels who in Baba's name dangle the carrot of experiences, boast about being able to communicate with Him, and control and manipulate innocent, trusting devotees.

Aai categorically warns devotees about this pitfall and asks devotees to pray to Baba directly. She asks them to practice their sadhana every day with discipline and regularity, putting Baba first in their lives.

Baba did emphasise that the path of self-realisation is not easy, and that certain prerequisites are essential for an aspirant just to be eligible to be on the spiritual path, let alone reach the end.

Firstly, for this a guide who has himself reached the end is needed. One has to pray for Baba's grace and He will guide the devotee, like He has in Aai's case since she is completely surrendered to Him. If He wishes, He may arrange for the devotee to reach a Master who would then bring the devotee to Baba.

Aai has seen countless devotees fall prey to people who have *siddhis* (paranormal powers) – such as the ability to read people's minds – and have taken advantage of trusting devotees saying that they get their guidance from Baba.

A clear sign of a Master, or a truly surrendered devotee like Aai, is that they have no need for you. One has to approach them with humility for they want nothing from you; it is truly the devotee who needs them and not the other way around.

Aai always says that we have been given intelligence, which we must use to discriminate between what is real and unreal, and not be foolish or have blind faith in anything or anyone. So it is important a devotee looks for these signs in anyone providing guidance and proceeds with caution.

If one is truly connected with Baba, one will experience peace and bliss, and become more like Him. Over time, one's needs will reduce and one will be content with what one has – needing nothing and wanting nothing from the world.

Conclusion – Everyone Can Have Baba's Experiences

Aai always says that she is not a special devotee and doesn't have any special powers granted by Baba. All that she has experienced can be experienced by one and all that do as she does.

In all humility, Aai always refers to herself as the dust of Baba's feet. Aai says that being regular with the sadhana and surrendering to Him completely will open the door to Baba taking over the welfare of the devotee.

It is Aai's promise to all that one who follows these steps will certainly experience His grace and Baba Himself will appear to that devotee!

It is by Baba's grace that we have been able to know of Aai, and by her example, be inspired in our love and devotion to Him. It is Baba Himself who operates through her, for she is the empty vessel that is completely surrendered to Him.

One is forever indebted to Baba, and His devotee Aai, for the love and grace He showers and bestows upon us. There is truly nothing we can ever do for Baba, but pray that our entire life is surrendered to His lotus feet, just as Aai's life is.

The Journey Of 'Sai Baba's Devotee Speaks'

While making a written record of Aai's life incidents for this book, one day Aai spontaneously told me, "You will meet many of Baba's close devotees and make an account of their experiences. This will help increase the devotion of numerous devotees and bring them closer to Baba."

Her words did stand out for me as I wondered to myself how I would meet such devotees and how this would unfold.

Shortly after this incident, when I was talking to Gautam, he mentioned it would be a good idea to record an interview with Aai in Marathi as she was getting older, and that it would be a treasure for devotees to draw inspiration from.

Things fell into place, we had someone fluent in Marathi, and who happened to be a devotee of Baba herself, come down to Goa and we recorded the first film titled 'Sai Baba's Devotee Speaks – An account of Baba's grace and miracles.'

We recorded a few more stories of Aai but I didn't know how to take the work further at the time.

A few months later, one evening, I was taking a walk down the beach, close to my home in Goa. All of a sudden, I spotted a small image of Lord Ganesha lying in the sand a little away from me. The image pulled me towards it as if by a magnetic force and I picked it up. At that time, I was not drawn to any specific form of God, but there was something within me that made me pick this image up. It was a small, shiny, green coloured sticker of Lord Ganesha, and I cleaned it, and reverently placed it in my car to take it home with me. After reaching home, I placed it on my desk and didn't think too much about it.

Strangely, about two weeks later, while I was at the other end of the same beach, I found another similar image of Lord Ganesha on the rock adjacent to me. It was almost as if the image had been placed there for me to pick it up. This one was also a sticker but red in colour. So I picked it up, cleaned it and took it home. By this time, I knew that this was no coincidence and that there had to be something more to it.

Every two weeks I used to also visit Aai since I lived quite close to her. On my next visit, I mentioned these two incidents and Aai spontaneously said, "Wait! A third one will come to you too!" I didn't think much about it at the time but her words stayed with me.

A few months passed after this meeting. I would visit the beach every evening to walk and practice silent meditation. One evening, while I was walking barefoot on the beach, I felt something under my toe. I could not see anything, so I moved the sand with my fingers and behold! It was a third image of Lord Ganesha, just as Aai had foretold! Even more mysteriously, it was an identical replica of the first image I had received on the same beach.

This wasn't during the festival of Ganesh Chaturthi, so it was very unusual to find stickers of Lord Ganesha of the same material, on the same beach, months apart!

I was blown away by Aai's all-knowingness and immediately called her. She said, "These are just the blessings of Lord Ganesha and Baba for you and any obstacles from your path will be removed."

As Aai had said, with Baba's grace, the work she had foretold I would undertake to spread Baba's name further started to unfold. The first special film we had recorded with Aai then became the foundation for the now very popular YouTube channel 'Sai Baba's Devotee Speaks', which has become a source of inspiration for countless devotees all across the globe

By Baba's blessings we continued to film a few intimate devotees like Aai and the channel now has a series of short films that record their experiences of Baba.

In addition to this, there are also films on Baba's history and teachings that preserve His sacred life and message. On this beautiful journey, Baba has shown His presence through numerous leelas and constantly guides the work, for it is He Himself who is getting this done for His devotees. We are just mere instruments in His hands.

The three images of Lord Ganesha found on the beach

We would encourage you to visit this sacred platform 'Sai Baba's Devotee Speaks' where devotees can watch all the films and access many other valuable resources.

The official website is www.MySaiBaba.com, where the films can be watched free of distraction and advertisements at the devotee's convenience. The channel is also on YouTube at www.youtube.com/SaiBabasDevoteeSpeaks or one could scan the code below to access the films.

Support Our Cause

'Sai Baba's Devotee Speaks' is comprised of a small group of devotees committed towards spreading the Divine teachings of Sai Baba through the production of films and publication of books such as this one.

In collaboration with Yogi Impressions, we have launched a new publication division called 'House of Sai'. This division will be dedicated towards bringing out numerous books to spread Baba's teachings and history further.

To ensure our books are accessible to devotees from all walks of life, we make them available at discounted rates. We subsidise the printing, production and distribution costs through the support we receive from our community. This division is run purely on a not-for-profit basis.

If you have been impacted by our work in any way and would like to help further our cause, we gladly welcome your support.

To support the work, please visit our website www.MySaiBaba.com/Support or scan the QR code below. We thank you in advance for your kind contribution.

Acknowledgements

My heartfelt gratitude to Aai, Masterjee, Rajendra (Aai's son-in-law) and their entire family for so wholeheartedly sharing their life stories and helping this book come to fruition; to Gautam Sachdeva for suggesting that we document Aai's story, which then became the founding stone of our channel, 'Sai Baba's Devotee Speaks'; to Tanushka Vaid for editing and helping structure the book; to my mother, Sunita, who patiently helped with the editing, captioning and translation of Aai's words from her interviews; and to all the patrons and supporters of the work that came together to help the channel take shape and become the platform it is today.

Snapshots From Aai And Masterjee's Life

Baba's photograph in Aai's old home

Aai

Masterjee

Young Aai with her two daughters

Aai, Masterjee and their family

Aai and Masterjee with some guests outside their old home

Aai and her family with Baba's shrine in their old home

Masterjee meditating

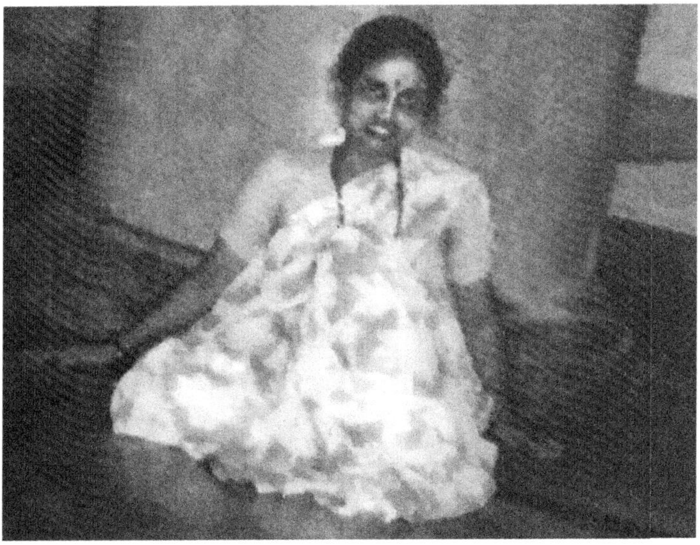

Aai sitting inside the temple

Aai and Masterjee in front of the small temple of Sai Baba at their home

A Humble Request From Aai And Masterjee

Over the past few years, numerous devotees have wished to meet Aai and Masterjee in person. However, due to their age and ailing health, it is no longer possible for them to do so.

Some devotees even find Aai and Masterjee's contact details and reach their home unannounced. They find it difficult to refuse anyone, and this takes a toll on their well-being.

Devotees initially ask Aai and Masterjee for a few minutes of their time but end up sitting for hours, without being sensitive of their health and limitations.

Thus, Aai requests devotees to simply follow the guidance shared by her and experience Baba's grace and intervention first-hand!

We thank you for your understanding.

Om Sai Ram.

For further details, contact:
Yogi Impressions LLP
1711, Centre 1, World Trade Centre,
Cuffe Parade, Mumbai 400 005, India.

Fill in the Mailing List form on our website and receive, via email, information on books, authors, events and more.
Visit: www.yogiimpressions.com

Telephone: (022) 22150207, 22155036
E-mail: yogi@yogiimpressions.com

Join us on Facebook:
www.facebook.com/yogiimpressions

Join us on Instagram:
www.instagram.com/yogi_impressions

ALSO PUBLISHED BY YOGI IMPRESSIONS

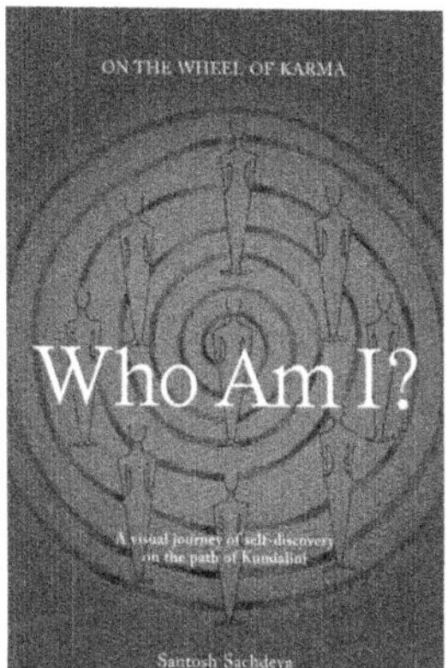

The Sacred India Tarot

Inspired by Indian Mythology and Epics

78 cards + 4 bonus cards + 350 page handbook

The Sacred India Tarot is truly an offering from India to the world. It is the first and only Tarot deck that works solely within the parameters of sacred Indian mythology – almost the world's only living mythology today.

Printed in Great Britain
by Amazon

85140854R00098